Boost Your
Interview IQ

Boost Your Interview IQ

Carole Martin

McGraw-Hill
New York Chicago San Francisco
Lisbon London Madrid Mexico City
Milan New Delhi San Juan Seoul
Singapore Sydney Toronto

9 0 FGR/FGR 0 9 8 7 6

ISBN 0-07-142547-0

McGraw-Hill books are available at special quantity discounts to use as premiums and sales promotions, or for use in corporate training programs. For more information, please write to the Director of Special Sales, McGraw-Hill Professional, Two Penn Plaza, New York, NY 10121-2298. Or contact your local bookstore.

 This book is printed on recycled, acid-free paper containing a minimum of 50% recycled, de-inked fiber.

Library of Congress Cataloging-in-Publication Data

Martin, Carole (Carole Hurd)
     Boost your interview IQ / Carole Martin.
          p.   cm.
     Includes index.
     ISBN 0-07-142547-0 (alk. paper)
     1. Interviewing.   I. Title.
     H61.28.M365   2004
     650.14'4—dc22

                                                2003017499

To Maurie, who believed in my ability and encouraged me to do what "I wanted to do."

To my daughter, Laura, who envisioned the future for my business.

To my son, Stan, who created the vision for me in a great website.

To my daughter, Julie, who was always there for me listening and encouraging me.

Contents

Acknowledgments

Thank you, thank you—

To Donya Dickerson, the best editor I could have asked for. Thanks for pulling and pushing and making this into the great book it is.

To Mariana French for the commas.

To Kim Isaacs, my guardian angel.

To Susan Harrow for her coaching and encouragement.

To Jennifer Robin for creating a great image and helping me improve my self-esteem.

To all the people I have interviewed, taught, and coached. You have taught me to be a better interviewer, coach, and person.

Foreword

The sweaty palms and racing pulse. The sickly feeling in your stomach that won't go away. The impending doom. No, it's not a walk to the electric chair—it's a job interview!

As the director of a resume-writing firm, I can attest to the number of hours that are poured into preparing an effective resume—the key document needed to land an interview. So when a coveted interview is granted, I'm surprised that many job seekers are content to "wing" the meeting and hope for the best.

In a perfect world, the most qualified candidate is offered the position. But that's not always the case, says Carole Martin—the job often goes to the applicant who has made the most favorable impression during the interview process. Carole will show you how to effectively prepare for job interviews so that you have the most likely chance of making a positive impression.

This book does not serve up stock answers to common interview questions, as this approach would make you seem stale and rehearsed. Rather, Carole teaches you how to write your personal success stories so that you're ready for just about any difficult question. Through an innovative "Interview IQ Test," you will learn why some answers to interview questions work while others do not. Then get ready to research your ideal job, understand the job's requirements, identify your key credentials, and write examples of your past accomplishments so that you may effectively sell your qualifications in an interview. You will learn to recognize different interview techniques so that you can better structure your responses. You will also learn what goes on behind the other side of the hiring desk, giving you a better understanding of what employers are looking for when interviewing candidates.

Carole's expertise in the field is unsurpassed. As Monster's Interview Coach and through her private coaching practice, Carole's dynamic approach has helped thousands ease the interview jitters, improve their interview finesse, and outperform their peers. I had the pleasure of attending one of Carole's workshops, where she taught her winning interview techniques to college students. I realized how lucky these students were to learn Carole's proven interview strategies toward the beginning of their careers.

As you embark on your job search, embrace Carole's interview strategies. Read and re-read the sample questions and answers, paying close attention to the reasoning behind why one answer is strongest and the others are somewhat lacking. Study this book and you'll find Carole sitting on your shoulder, guiding you throughout the interview and ensuring that you are making a positive impression.

Boost Your Interview IQ is an insightful guide that will help anyone trying to improve his or her interview performance. Whether you're new to interviewing or a seasoned pro, you'll find great advice and adaptable techniques that will improve your confidence, enable you to "sell" yourself during interviews, and produce more job offers.

—Kim Isaacs
Director of ResumePower.com, Monster's Resume Expert,
and coauthor of *The Career Change Resume*
Doylestown, PA

Introduction

A Breakthrough System for Showing That You Are the Best Person for the Job

This book is your passport to acing any interview. You'll learn to tell any interviewer not only that you can do the job but that you are the best person for the job. After working with the techniques presented throughout this book, you will be able to tell any interviewer confidently how you will bring your experiences from the past with you to the job and how you are *the* candidate that company wants to hire. It's a tough job market out there, and being able to show the interviewer that you are the best person for the job is essential. Otherwise, you will lose out to the competition and another person will get the job.

By learning these interviewing techniques, you will obtain the tools that will prepare you to answer interview questions that have stumped you in the past. Some of the most difficult questions to answer are those which ask for specific examples. Whenever interviewers ask for examples or ask questions that begin with "Tell me about a time when," they are seeking a *specific* example to see how you work—in other words, your method of operation. The formal name for this method of questioning is "behavioral interviewing." What this means is that the person interviewing you is trying to learn how you performed in the past. Your examples in your answers will be used to ascertain whether you have what it takes to do the job for the company. As the interviewers listen to your examples and stories, they begin to notice patterns in your behavior that help them determine whether you have the experience you claim to have on your résumé.

> **Myth:** The best candidate always gets the job!
> **Reality:** The candidate who sells himself or herself most effectively always gets the job!

One of the goals of this book is to teach you, through the use of models, how to write examples and stories that will help you demonstrate that you have the experience needed to do the job. In subsequent parts of this book you will learn to use the models to prepare your own stories in a way that will demonstrate clearly the skills and accomplishments you have, specifically those pertaining to the job you are interviewing for, and persuade the employer that you have "been there and done that"—and can do it again!

Selling Yourself as a Product

Interviewing is about selling. In a job interview you sell yourself as a solution to the hiring manager's problem.

It's a straightforward process:

An employer has a problem: work to be done. The first step the employer takes is to define what qualifications are necessary: a "wish list" for the type of person who best fits the position. A posting is entered on the Internet or an ad is placed in the newspaper with the hope of finding the "best" person for the job. In a normal job market an employer will settle for a match of 80 percent of the requirements; when the job market is tight, the employer has such a vast selection of candidates to choose from that the percentage rises to 100 percent and then some. In these kinds of market conditions people giving interviews frequently ask, "What else do you have to offer in addition to the basics required?"

You, as the job seeker, see the ad or posting and know that you are the perfect person for the job. You have most or all of the qualifications and know that you can do the job. You submit your résumé and wait for the phone call to be invited for an interview so that you can convince the employer that you are the solution to the problem and the best person for the job.

When you receive the call inviting you to an interview, you are delighted.

It would be nice if the excitement lasted and you sailed through the interview process and got a job offer every time. However, life is not that simple, and neither is the interviewing process.

Often your initial excitement turns to fear and then to panic. "What if I don't have all the answers to the questions?" you ask yourself. "They probably will choose another candidate because things never work out for me," you tell yourself. "If only I didn't have to go through the interview process; I know I can do that job," you say to yourself.

All these feelings of questioning and self-doubt are normal. In fact, they are extremely normal. Most people *hate* interviewing. It's a judgment process, and who wants to go through that and face the possibility of a rejection?

By using the tools in this book and learning the specific interview story-telling techniques, you will begin to feel more in control and confident about going to your next interview. Instead of feeling that you are bragging about yourself, you will be focusing on what you have to offer and letting the interviewer know that you are not only qualified but are the best person for the job! In Part I, the Interview IQ Test and the sections that follow will guide you in preparing your own stories and examples. Being prepared with your success stories will make a tremendous difference in the way you feel about interviewing.

By taking the Interview IQ Test and rating your ability to judge the strongest answers, you will see how good you are at judging what the interviewer will be interested in hearing. You then can write your own stories as a way to tell interviewers about your own experiences and back up your claims and statements.

Once you understand how to give an example of past behavior with an interesting story, you will be able to prove to the interviewer that you have the relevant experience that company wants in the person it will hire. When you have written stories that are specific and focused, you will feel more prepared and confident. That means more successful interviews—and more job offers.

Although the emphasis of this book is on the candidate, the information is appropriate for anyone desiring an in-depth, experiential approach to the interviewing process.

FEELING PREPARED = IMPROVED CONFIDENCE =
SUCCESSFUL INTERVIEW = JOB OFFER

How to Improve Your Interviewing Skills, Particularly with Behavioral Questions

More and more interviewers are using a technique called behavioral interviewing. In fact, according to the website for the Career Services center at the SUNY College at Brockport, more than 30 percent of companies now use behavioral interviewing as their preferred way to choose top candidates.

What this means is that interviewers interpret what you say about yourself and your past behavior as an indicator of how you will behave in the future. In other words, if you did it before, you can do it again. It is in your best interest to be able to demonstrate through the use of recent, relevant examples that you have done similar jobs with proven success. When the interviewer begins to see patterns and hear about successes on your past jobs, you will be considered a serious candidate for the job.

What differentiates behavioral questions from traditional interview questions is the way the question is asked.

Traditional Question

"What would you do if you had to deal with an angry customer?"

A traditional interview question gives you the chance to spin a fairy tale. You can use your imagination and tell a wonderful tale to answer this type of question.

It is quite different when the interviewer asks a behavioral question.

Behavioral Question

"You say you have 'great customer service skills.' Can you give me an example of a time when you had to deal with an angry customer?"

You now have the challenge of thinking about your past experiences and coming up with a specific example of a time when you dealt with an angry customer. If you have been in a customer service position, you may have too many stories to deal with. This is when preparation makes the difference and pays off. In Part 2 you will learn to read through a job posting/description and pick out the "key factors" that will help you prepare your stories ahead of time, selecting those which make you look like the best person for the job.

> The key to answering behavioral questions successfully is to be as specific as possible, particularly in relation to the position you are seeking.

Below is a warm-up exercise to get you ready to take the Interview IQ Test. A behavioral question is asked, and three possible answers are given: (A), (B), and (C). It is your task to pick the answer you think is the *strongest* one. Put yourself in the role of the interviewer and try to determine which answer would impress you the most.

Exercise: A Sample Text Question

INTERVIEWER'S QUESTION

"Tell me about a time when you had to deal with an angry customer."
  Select the strongest answer.

(A) A woman called and was yelling about a product that didn't work. I listened and let her vent. I then made sure that I understood all the facts and told her that I would call her back within the next two hours. I did some research and found that her product was still under warranty and that we could send her a replacement product at no charge. I called her back, and she was glad to hear that. She thanked me and asked for my supervisor's name so that she could report my efficient service.

(B) Since I work in customer service, this happens every day. Someone calls and yells at me, and I have to take it. Sometimes I can help the customer by making a suggestion or referring the customer somewhere else, but not always. I just try to stay calm and not get irritated. I know that the customers aren't yelling at me and that they are really frustrated. I try to help as much as I can.

(C) Every time I get one of these angry people, I have to just sit and listen. Some days it is difficult to hear all the complaints, but that's the nature of the job. I just try not to take it personally and get through the day.

ANSWERS
The Strongest Answer

(A) This answer is the strongest one because it provides a specific example of your experience dealing with an angry customer. The interviewer can recognize through your example skills that are relevant to the job: communication, listening skills, good customer service skills, patience, the ability to research facts, and good follow-through.

The Mediocre Answer

(B) This is not as strong an answer because it lacks an example. The interviewer may sense a good work ethic and attitude but doesn't hear an example of how you handled a stressful situation or learn about any experiences you have had in dealing with customers. This represents a missed opportunity.

The Weakest Answer

(C) This is the weakest answer because it has a negative tone; it is almost whiny. It does not demonstrate an attitude that is supportive of customer service and does not offer any examples of the skills you have used to deal with situations like this one. The interviewer does not learn how you deal with customers from this answer.

RATE YOURSELF

If you chose answer (A), give yourself 5 points.

If you chose answer (B), give yourself 3 points.

If you chose answer (C), give yourself 0 points.   5

As you can see, the impression you make as a result of the story is more important than the story itself. Interviewers listen for skills and behavior to see if you can do the job and if your résumé claims can be backed up. Interviewers will not always remember the answers, but they will remember the impressions the answers made. By giving a specific answer, one that directly answers the question asked, you will give an impression of someone who not only has the needed skills but also follows directions. In Part 2 you will learn techniques to make your stories as interesting and as focused as possible.

The Interview IQ Test

Do you get the idea of the story and why it is important? Are you ready to try your hand at selecting the strongest answers by taking the Interview IQ Test? If so, it's time to move on to the next step.

Go through the questions, add up the points, and check your score. This is not a test in the sense that you will pass or fail. It is an exercise to help you recognize the mistakes you might be making when answering questions and to help you prepare stronger answers in the future. It is a test to be taken over and over again, each time improving your sense of what makes a story stronger and boosting your Interview IQ.

Turn the page and begin to take the Interview IQ Test.

Always select what you determine to be the *strongest* answer. The best way to benefit from the exercise is to think the way an interviewer might think. Reading through the example, would you want to hear more from this person as a possible candidate for your job? Which answer impresses you the most?

After completing the test, rate yourself and your ability to select the *strongest* answers. Add up the points you have accumulated from each question answered and record your score. See pages 115–118 for a scorecard you can use again and again. When you have your total points, check your rating. Remember that this is a test that can be retaken until you get the score you desire.

PART 1

The Interview
IQ Test

Test Your Interview IQ–
Questions and Answers

Take the Test and Rate
Your Interviewing Ability

If you take the Interview IQ Test, you will have a measure of how you size up when answering some of the most frequently asked interview questions.

Whether you are new to interviewing or have had a lot of interviewing experience, the Interview IQ Test will give you a deeper understanding of what is involved in the questions from the interviewer's perspective. Even if you are "interview-savvy," reading through the test will give you an updated perspective on current interviewing practices.

As in any book on interviewing, the answers provided are not meant to be memorized and recited at an interview, resulting in canned- or robotic-sounding answers. You will have far more successful interviews if you answer the questions in a sincere and natural manner, giving the interviewer an opportunity to get to know you and hear how you work best. That does not mean going into the interview and "winging it." It means being prepared with your own answers, which will make you feel confident and able to present what you have to offer.

Canned answers are easy for an interviewer to spot because they sound like something anyone could say.

Interviewer's Question: "What are you looking for in your next job?"

Canned Answer: "I want to work for a growth-oriented company where I can utilize my skills and learn and develop new skills."

IQ Test Instructions

After each Interviewer's Question there are three possible answers to choose from: (A), (B), and (C). It is your task to select the answer you think would be most effective in an interview situation. Choose the answer you think is the *strongest*. As you read through the choices, think the way the interviewer might think. Which answer provides an in-depth look at the candidate's skills and experiences?

When you've completed the test, check the answers that follow and assign yourself the points indicated next to your choice. The next step is to total your points and check your Interview Ability Rating.

Regardless of how you rate, take the test a second time and see if you can *boost* your Interview IQ score. By reading the examples several times you will become comfortable with the types of questions you may encounter and get an idea of the strongest answers to those questions. For a scorecard to use as you answer each question, see pages 115–118. This scorecard can be used every time you take the Interview IQ Test.

> Try rereading the Interview IQ Test the day before your next interview to refresh your memory on what makes an answer the strongest one.

When you feel satisfied that you have the hang of the technique and that your score is as high as you want it to be, you will be ready to start preparing your own stories. For instructions on creating your own answers, turn to Part 2 to learn the secrets of the trade and get an in-depth look at storytelling that will make it easier for you to write your own focused and concise stories.

The Test: The Fifty Most Frequently Asked Interview Questions

The following interview questions have been divided into two categories: general questions (the first 25) and behavioral questions (the next 25). When you read through the questions and answers, you will get a sense of what differentiates a question as behavioral and the technique needed to answer this type of question. You will find that there are no "right" or "wrong" answers, but you will begin to see how some answers are stronger and more effective than others.

General Interview Questions

General questions are the questions most commonly used in interviews. There are no guarantees that these will be the specific questions asked in an interview, but if you are able to answer these basic questions, you will be able to answer most other questions with greater ease. These are "getting to know you" questions. This is where the interviewer gets to know your skills, strengths, weaknesses, motivators, and style. These questions also include information about what motivates you and when you have been satisfied in your work. In other words, they ask, "Who are you?" "What are you looking for?" and "How would you fit in here?"

Turn the page for the general section of the Interview IQ Test.

INTERVIEWER'S QUESTION

1. **"Let's begin with you telling me about yourself."**
   Select the strongest answer.

   (A) I was born in Cincinnati. My mother was a nurse, and my father was a lawyer. I went to the local high school and then attended the state college and graduated with a major in English. I worked for four years at a high-tech company, where I was a customer service rep. Then I moved to a large company and worked there for two years as a help desk rep. I was at my last company for one year as a manager of customer service.

   (B) I have a total of seven years in the customer service field. In my last job I managed a team of 14 reps. I have excellent communication and interpersonal skills, and that allows me to work with a broad range of people at various levels. My background includes working in Fortune 500 companies as well as smaller companies. My strength is my ability to organize and coordinate projects, making sure deadlines are met.

   (C) I'd be glad to. Would you like to know about my personal life or my professional life? What would you like me to focus on?

ANSWERS
The Strongest Answer

(B) This is the strongest answer because it presents a good summary of what you have to offer. The interviewer knows your total years of experience, the types of companies where you have worked, and what you consider your strengths relative to the job. The answer also provides a good blend of knowledge-based skills, transferable skills, and some personality traits. You are striving to give the interviewer a good snapshot of yourself.

The Mediocre Answer

(A) This answer is all right but is not as strong an answer (B). This is basically a "walk-through-the-résumé" type of answer: "I was born, attended college, and worked at…." It would benefit from more detail and specifics, such as the types of companies you worked for or some of your strengths and personal characteristics. The ideal answer contains a well-rounded, current picture of you.

The Weakest Answer

(C) This is a very common reply to this question but is a weak answer. It does not show any preparation or planning in regard to what the employer would be interested in knowing about you. Your reply to this question is your opportunity to lead the interview and start out by focusing on what you want the interviewer to know about you and your qualifications for the position.

RATE YOURSELF

If you chose answer **(B)**, give yourself 5 points.

If you chose answer **(A)**, give yourself 3 points.

If you chose answer **(C)**, give yourself 0 points.   _____

INTERVIEWER'S QUESTION

2. "Why did you leave (or why are you planning to leave) your last position?"

Select the strongest answer.

(A) The company had a reorganization, and my department was eliminated. The work had begun to dwindle, and so it was not a complete surprise. I liked my job and the people I was working with, so I had been hoping that it wouldn't affect us, but unfortunately, we were all let go. I would like to find a job similar to the one I lost.

(B) I am looking for a new challenge. I have been with my current company for two years now and don't find the work as interesting as I once did. I am looking for a company where I can take on new challenges and grow. My current job is a dead end for me.

(C) Since there are no advancement opportunities within the company, I have decided that it would be a good time for me to look outside. I have set some career goals for myself and could not achieve them at that company. What I am looking for is a job with a bigger company where I can contribute but also move on a career path that has more responsibility.

ANSWERS
The Strongest Answer

(A) This is the strongest answer not because of the layoff but because it has an upbeat tone. You liked what you did and were hoping the layoff wouldn't happen. In other words, if it hadn't been for something out of your control, you would still be there. The answer indicates a good attitude toward an unfortunate incident.

The Mediocre Answer

(C) This is an acceptable answer. It is natural to want to take on more responsibility; it is also acceptable to quit a job. A skilled interviewer would follow up with a question about your career goals and why you think you can achieve them at the new company. Would you have an answer prepared for that question?

The Weakest Answer

(B) This is the weakest answer because it is trite. One of the most common answers to this question is that you are "looking for a challenge." An interviewer might be concerned that if you were bored at your last job, you will find this job boring as well, or at least not "challenging" enough.

RATE YOURSELF

If you chose answer **(A)**, give yourself 5 points.

If you chose answer **(C)**, give yourself 3 points.

If you chose answer **(B)**, give yourself 0 points.   _____

INTERVIEWER'S QUESTION

3. **"Why do you want to work here?"**
   Select the strongest answer.

   (A) I did some research and selected the companies I am most interested in working for, and yours is at the top of my list. I conducted my research on the basis of the company's reputation,
   product reliability, and industry stability, as well as how current
   employees would rate working for the company. I work best
   when my goals and values are in sync with the company's goals
   and values. I know that I would be a good fit in this company's
   culture and that I have a lot to contribute.

   (B) I found the job posting on the Internet. The job is a perfect match
   for my skills and abilities. I see this as a real opportunity to find
   a challenge. I want to work for a company where I can grow and
   develop and be challenged. I am looking for a company with a
   solid financial record and industry standing—like yours. I know
   I would fit in here and be able to "put down roots."

   (C) When I saw the ad in the paper, I knew this was the job for me. I
   have always been a fan of your clothing line and buy at your
   stores all the time. I would really like to be able to say I work for
   this company. It's important to me that the company I work for
   have a good reputation and good products. I see this as a great
   opportunity for me to be with a top-notch company that I really
   feel good about.

ANSWERS

The Strongest Answer

(A) This is the strongest answer, because it demonstrates planning and control on your part, not just an attitude of "there was an opening and I thought I would apply." You demonstrate that you have given some thought to what you want and how to go about getting it. You selected this company by doing research and checking out how employees rate the company. This answer shows confidence in your skills and ability to fit into the culture. A caution would involve the way this answer is delivered. Overconfidence can be as big a turnoff as lack of confidence.

The Mediocre Answer

(C) This is a very mediocre answer. It emphasizes "you" and what you can get from the opportunity. While being a fan or customer of a company is good from the consumer point of view, the answer would be stronger if you looked at the business side of the situation, for instance, by talking about one of your favorite ads or marketing campaigns used by the company or how the company is doing against its competitors—something that indicates how your role as a consumer relates to the job you are applying for. Simply being a fan or customer of a company does not get you any extra points in the interview process. A little flattery goes a long way, but make sure you are looking at the business side of the picture, not the consumer side.

The Weakest Answer

(B) This is the weakest answer. The emphasis is on "what's in it for you—finding a challenge and growing and developing." The bottom line of the interview process is "What can you do for this company?" not "What can the company can do for you?"

RATE YOURSELF

If you chose answer (A), give yourself 5 points.

If you chose answer (C), give yourself 3 points.

If you chose answer (B), give yourself 0 points.   _____

INTERVIEWER'S QUESTION

4. **"What are your goals?"**

   Select the strongest answer.

   (A) My goal is to work for a company where I can grow and eventually become a marketing manager. I would like to lead a team of "handpicked" people and have a major impact on the company. I am interested in a company that is forward-thinking and growth-oriented.

   (B) I want to work in a department that believes in cross-functional training. I think that is the best way to learn and see the bigger picture in a company. Eventually I hope to return to school to earn an MBA. I think that will broaden my knowledge so that one day I can own my own consultant company, working nationally or internationally.

   (C) I break down goals into short-term goals, with the long term in mind. Right now I'm looking for a position in a company with a solid track record. I want to contribute to a team, bringing my extensive experience in this field to add to the team mix. Long-term goals will depend on the career path available at the company. Ideally, I would like to move progressively within a company.

ANSWERS

The Strongest Answer

(C) This is the strongest answer among the three choices. Since this an open-ended question, there is no right or wrong way to answer it. This answer is the best because it is open to opportunities that allow room for growth but doesn't lock the speaker into goals that may not be realistic or are too rigid or specific.

The Mediocre Answer

(A) The problem with this answer is that it is too specific and could be a turndown factor if the company does not have a career path that would allow an employee to reach this goal. It is best to stay away from answers that are narrow or inflexible.

The Weakest Answer

(B) This answer starts out well and then takes a nosedive. While it pays to be honest, this answer could turn the interviewer off. The employer is looking for someone who will stick around and contribute to the company. It is not the company's goal to hire someone and train that person to become a competitor one day.

RATE YOURSELF

If you chose answer (C), give yourself 5 points.

If you chose answer (A), give yourself 3 points.

If you chose answer (B), give yourself 0 points.   _____

INTERVIEWER'S QUESTION

5. **"What are your strengths?"**

    Select the strongest answer.

    (A) My strength is my strong people skills. I love working with people and helping them solve problems. My customers are very important to me, and I let them know it. I've had a lot of positive feedback on my skills from my customers.

    (B) My strengths are a combination of my technical skills and my ability to work with a variety of customers. I consider myself a data-mining expert, but what makes me stand out from the competition is my ability to work directly with customers and get to the root of the problem. I can break down complex issues into simple, understandable concepts and language so that the customers can understand what I am saying. I have received customer service awards in the technical area for the last two years.

    (C) I have a strong background in customer service. Whether the customer is internal or external, I pride myself on my ability to work with people on problems and solutions. I've been chosen for the "Customer Service of the Month" award every quarter for the last two years.

ANSWERS

The Strongest Answer

(B) This is the strongest answer because it gives a broader picture of what you bring to the position: not only what is required—technical skills—but also the added value of being able to work directly with the customer as well as a strong ability to communicate technical information in simple terms. In today's competitive market it will be necessary for you to think of your strengths beyond meeting the qualifications. What else can you offer that other candidates cannot? The more skills you can include in your answer, the more information the interviewer will have to judge whether you have what it takes to do the job—and beyond.

The Mediocre Answer

(C) This is not as strong an answer as (B). It is good in that it lets the interviewer know that you have a strong ability to work with internal and external customers and work with problems and solutions. This answer would be stronger if you blended in some of the skills that come from your experience or knowledge, such as your industry or product knowledge.

The Weakest Answer

(A) This is a very general answer that could be used for any position. "I love working with people" and "I am a people person" are overused phrases. Helping people solve problems is too general a concept to make a good impression on the interviewer.

RATE YOURSELF

If you chose answer (B), give yourself 5 points.

If you chose answer (C), give yourself 3 points.

If you chose answer (A), give yourself 0 points.   _____

A good way to prepare for the "strengths" question is to do an assessment of what you have to offer. This means not only your knowledge-based skills (experience and education) but also the skills that are used in almost any job—transferable or portable skills (communication skills, time management skills, problem-solving skills).

INTERVIEWER'S QUESTION

6. **"What is your greatest weakness?"**
   Select the strongest answer.

   (A) Weaknesses are not something that I dwell on. I know I could improve on my patience when working with people who don't work at the same pace as I do. What I have found is that by helping members of the team who are having problems, I can move projects forward instead of being frustrated and doing nothing.

   (B) I am a person who likes to get the job done correctly the first time. I become very frustrated when other people's work affects my ability to do my job correctly. I've been working on trying to be more understanding and finding out what the problem is before I pass judgment.

   (C) My weakness is working too hard to get the job done. Because of the workload, I have to work many evenings and weekends so that projects meet deadlines. I'm trying to work smarter and not harder.

ANSWERS
The Strongest Answer

(A) This answer comes across as being very sincere and honest. Some forethought was put into the answer. It also shows an awareness of your need to improve and what action steps you need to take to work through the issue.

The Mediocre Answer

(B) This is not a bad answer. However, the interviewer could become concerned that you are a bit of a perfectionist, and that could cause a problem. Avoid mentioning personality traits that would be difficult to change. In answering this question it is best to demonstrate something you are working on to improve your weakness: "I'm working on it."

The Weakest Answer

(C) This is a very trite answer and should be avoided. "Working too hard" is a concept that even the cartoons have had some fun with. An interviewer might be concerned about whether you are working hard because of the workload or because of poor work habits.

RATE YOURSELF

If you chose answer **(A),** give yourself 5 points.

If you chose answer **(B),** give yourself 3 points.

If you chose answer **(C),** give yourself 0 points.   _____

The "weakness" question is the *most* dreaded question of all. In answering this question it is best to avoid saying that you are weak in any areas that would affect your job performance (as seen in the job positing). For example, "My time management skills need some improving" would be a poor thing to say because you are admitting that you may not be able to do the job.

INTERVIEWER'S QUESTION

7. **"When have you been most motivated?"**
   Select the strongest answer.

   (A) In my previous job I worked directly with customers and their problems. What I liked was solving problems and helping people. Sometimes it was difficult because of the people constantly complaining and being upset with me. I would try not to take it personally, but I'll admit there were times when it was a challenge. What motivated me was when customers took the time to tell me they appreciated the service.

   (B) Last year I was involved in a project that was very exciting. I was assigned to work with a team, and we had to brainstorm about a product that was not being received well by the consumers. I would wake up in the morning thinking of creative ways to overcome our problem. The especially great part of this project was the team I was working with. The team and the creative problem solving are what make a difference in my motivation.

   (C) I'm pretty motivated all the time. I feel really good about solving problems for the customer. I like the challenge of a new problem and the chance to think of ways to solve problems. I'm really unmotivated when all I have are pieces of someone else's problem to clean up. I like taking a project from the beginning to the end.

ANSWERS

The Strongest Answer

(B) This is the strongest answer because it is the most specific. You can get a strong sense of the enthusiasm and energy behind the motivation and satisfaction. Think about the time when you were last motivated. How did it feel?

The Mediocre Answer

(A) This answer tends to emphasize the negative aspects of the job almost as much as the motivating or positive side of the job. It would be a stronger answer if you talked only about helping people and solving problems, especially times when the people appreciated your service.

The Weakest Answer

(C) This is the weakest of the three answers because almost anyone could say these things. This answer also takes a negative turn when it begins to focus on being "unmotivated." Since that was not part of the question, it is not a good idea to volunteer information that might be interpreted as complaining about mundane tasks, which are part of most jobs.

RATE YOURSELF

If you chose answer **(B),** give yourself 5 points.

If you chose answer **(A),** give yourself 3 points.

If you chose answer **(C),** give yourself 0 points.   _____

INTERVIEWER'S QUESTION

8. **"How would you describe your personality?"**

   Select the strongest answer.

   (A) I am a high-energy person who is a hard worker. I learn very quickly and adapt well. I am very responsible about deadlines. I have the ability to get along well with people. I have a very upbeat attitude that helps keep the department's morale up. I have the ability to get along well with everyone.

   (B) I am a high-energy person who is motivated by new challenges and problems. I can hit the ground running and come up to speed faster than anyone I know. I have a proven record of success and a reputation for meeting deadlines on time. My attitude about work is "whatever it takes to get the job done." Anyone in my department would tell you that I am someone who really supports the team spirit.

   (C) I'm a problem solver who is a whiz at analyzing data and transforming it into useful information. My strength is my ability to convert complex details into simple understandable language. I have been able to save companies time and money by coming up with solutions.

ANSWERS

The Strongest Answer

(B) This is the strongest answer because of the energy it demonstrates. This answer describes your personality in a unique manner: not just a hard worker with a good attitude but an adaptable person with a "whatever it takes to get the job done" attitude. This is followed by an endorsement from your fellow workers of your ability to be a "team player."

The Mediocre Answer

(A) There is nothing in this answer that makes you unique. If you compare the words in answer (B) with those in answer (A), you will notice that they basically say the same thing. The difference is the added "zip." The terms used in this answer are trite. A high percentage of people would answer with "hard worker." If you do say you are a hard worker, it would be a stronger answer if you referred to a time when you worked above and beyond what was called for: "I often work 10-hour days." Overall this answer needs some punch.

The Weakest Answer

(C) This answer refers more to skills than to your personality. It has a strong focus on analytical problem solving but is one-dimensional. By adding some personality traits that are more transferable, such as communication skills, you would give a better, well-rounded picture of yourself.

RATE YOURSELF

If you chose answer (B), give yourself 5 points.

If you chose answer (A), give yourself 3 points.

If you chose answer (C), give yourself 0 points.   _____

Describing your personality is like writing an ad for a product. What makes you unique? Making a list of your specific personality traits is a good exercise to prepare for an interview.

INTERVIEWER'S QUESTION

9. "Have you ever been fired?"
Select the strongest answer.

(A) I accepted my last job partly because I had a good rapport with my boss. After I was there six months, she left the company. From the very beginning it was clear that my new boss and I were going to be at odds. We just had different personality types. She kept changing the rules. One day she would want it this way, and the next day she'd want it another way. This woman was really overbearing in her management approach. One day she called me in and told me I was fired, with no explanation. She just fired me!

(B) One of the managers who reported to me made a big mistake that caused the company to lose a great deal of money. Because I was his boss, we were both fired. At first I did not think this was fair. I now realize that the man was under my supervision and that it was on my shift, and I take full responsibility for what happened. I have put the incident behind me and am looking forward to moving on to new opportunities.

(C) I made a mistake in judgment that went against company policy and was fired. I'm not proud of what I did and was hard on myself about the mistake, but I also learned a lot from the incident. There is no point holding on to the past. I will be more careful about my actions in the future. I am ready for a second chance and know that I will be a better employee because of this experience.

ANSWERS

The Strongest Answer

(B) This is the strongest answer because of the honesty and wisdom of accepting things that are out of your control and taking responsibility. Being able to look the interviewer in the eye and admit you made a mistake is not easy, but it may pay off in the long run.

The Mediocre Answer

(C) This answer is straightforward and truthful. Laying the truth on the table is a better way of handling the situation than is lying because one lie leads to another. The way you deliver this answer will be as important as the answer itself. You broke company policy. Some employers will not take a chance on you once you've been fired. However, there will be those who appreciate your honesty and sincerity and may see this as an honorable trait.

The Weakest Answer

(A) This is the weakest answer because the blame is put on someone else. Even though this was out of your control and you feel you didn't deserve to be fired, it is not a good idea to berate management. It is best to say that when the boss who hired you left, the position changed and it was no longer a good fit with your values and goals. If you are questioned further, you can say that your new boss had a work style different from yours.

RATE YOURSELF

If you chose answer **(B)**, give yourself 5 points.

If you chose answer **(C)**, give yourself 3 points

If you chose answer **(A)**, give yourself 0 points.   _____

People get fired every day. They move on and get new jobs. No matter what the circumstances, it is best to put it behind you. Deal with your feelings about the firing before the interview, and as you prepare your script, you will feel more confident and less emotional about the situation.

INTERVIEWER'S QUESTION

10. **"Why has it taken you so long to find a job?"**
    Select the strongest answer.

    (A) Because the job market is so tight, I did not run out and try to get just any job. I took my time, thinking about finding the "right" job. I went on some informational interviews to find out what opportunities were out there and where this industry was headed. I also took some on-line classes and a few short courses. I have to admit it was a nice time to research and explore. I now feel prepared and ready to find the right opportunity.

    (B) I'm really not sure. I have an excellent background with five years of experience in this industry and knowledge of several software programs. I know there are a lot of other people out there with similar skills, but what sets me apart from the masses is my ability to relate and work with a wide range of customers. Having the combination of technical skills and people skills has helped me advance. I am looking for an opportunity in a company that respects customer service.

    (C) It's a really tight job market out there, and it just hasn't been easy to get a job. I have been in a job search the entire time. I just didn't get lucky. I did all the right things like networking and going to job clubs and meetings, but my skills just didn't seem to be in demand. I know there are a lot of people out there looking. The competition is tough.

ANSWERS

The Strongest Answer

> **(B)** This is the most honest answer. It also deflects the question and focuses on what you have to offer, especially what separates you from all the other people applying for this job. Talking about what you can bring to the job, not what you have gone through to get to this interview is a good technique.

The Mediocre Answer

> **(A)** This is a fairly good answer because it explains what you have been doing in the time you've been unemployed. It could benefit from some information about what you have discovered in your quest for information or what you have to offer as a result of your searching.

The Weakest Answer

> **(C)** This is the weakest answer because it blames the economy for your "bad luck." It also talks about your skills not being in demand instead of describing what you did to improve your skills to make yourself more employable. This answer has a somewhat passive tone. An interviewer might get the idea that no one else was willing to hire you and that maybe you are not a desirable product.

RATE YOURSELF

If you chose answer **(B)**, give yourself 5 points.

If you chose answer **(A)**, give yourself 3 points.

If you chose answer **(C)**, give yourself 0 points.   _____

INTERVIEWER'S QUESTION

11. **"What experience do you have that qualifies you for this position?"**
    Select the strongest answer.

    (A) My experience is a good match with the qualifications needed for this position. I meet all your requirements and then some. I think I could bring added value to this position through my understanding and knowledge of international business in Asian countries. Speaking the language and understanding the cultural norms would be a tremendous asset in negotiations and dealings with companies from those countries.

    (B) I know I could do this job. I have the skills and experience necessary to succeed here. I want to work for this company, and I feel that this position would be an opportunity and a challenge for me. I am a person who likes to be challenged, and I also intend to continue to grow and learn new skills. I am strong at solving problems using analytical data. I like working on a team and contributing to solutions.

    (C) With six years of experience working in the electronics industry, I have worked on the types of systems required for this job. My strength is my leadership skills. I have supervised technicians and testers on a 24/7 schedule. If you asked my staff members about me, they would tell you that I was there when they needed me. I am very adaptable and have worked as many as 70 hours in a week so that we could meet a deadline.

ANSWERS
The Strongest Answer

(C) This is the strongest answer. The answer gives a broad picture of you and how your skills would fill the interviewer's needs. It gives examples of strengths in the area of technology, leadership skills (which are considered transferable skills), and your willingness to do "whatever it takes to get the job done." The "third-party endorsement" from the people who have worked with you is very helpful. Speaking through others' comments is a strong technique to use when you are answering questions.

The Mediocre Answer

(A) This answer has its strong points, but it does not present as good an overall picture as answer (C) does. Any time you can speak of bringing "added value" to a company, whether through languages, people skills, or the ability to do something that most candidates cannot, you should sell it as a strong point. Depending on how important your value is to the position, this could make the difference in your being the chosen candidate.

The Weakest Answer

(B) This answer focuses too much on what the job can do for *you*. The emphasis is best placed on what you can do for *the company*. This answer would be stronger if it gave specific information about the years of experience and the types of problems solved.

RATE YOURSELF

If you chose answer (C), give yourself 5 points.

If you chose answer (A), give yourself 3 points.

If you chose answer (B), give yourself 0 points.   _____

INTERVIEWER'S QUESTION

12. **"How would your current or last boss describe your job perfor-mance?"**

    Select the strongest answer.

    (A) My last boss and I had very different personalities, and that sometimes resulted in conflicts. I think he would tell you that I was above all a professional in all my dealings with customers, internal and external. He also would tell you that I met all my deadlines.

    (B) She would tell you that I was her "right-hand man." She would make the decisions, and I did the background and technical work—she relied on me to do all the calculations and data input on projects. I kept her on track when she was running behind schedule, and I jumped in when she needed a hand. She would tell you that I was still her friend even though it's been five years since we worked together.

    (C) He would tell you that I have excellent skills working with all kinds of people. He nominated me for an in-service award for my excellent customer service work within the company. He treated me with respect and gave me the feedback I needed to learn and grow in my job. He also would tell you that I was very depend-able and always made my deadlines.

ANSWERS

The Strongest Answer

(B) This is the stronger answer because it gives clear picture of the way you work with authority: supportive and responsible. This answer informs the interviewer about your technical skills and abilities as well as your flexibility and willingness. It also speaks of the relationship you built with your boss. Not all jobs end with personal relationships, but if you can quote your boss or mention something positive that a boss said in a performance review, it will strengthen your answer.

The Mediocre Answer

(C) This is an acceptable answer but is not as strong as answer **(B)** because it is not as specific. It points out good communication and people skills as well as your being dependable and meeting deadlines, which is good, but it would benefit from an example. The fact that you were nominated for an award is definitely worth mentioning.

The Weakest Answer

(A) This is a weak answer. It's best to avoid talking about differences in a negative way. Although this answer does not really "bad-mouth" the employer, it points out that there was a problem. The interviewer's concern would be that you did not get along well with your bosses. The answer does have a positive slant because it talks about being professional and meeting deadlines. A good interviewer would probe further and find out the nature of the conflicts.

RATE YOURSELF

If you chose answer **(B)**, give yourself 5 points.

If you chose answer **(C)**, give yourself 3 points.

If you chose answer **(A)**, give yourself 0 points.   _____

INTERVIEWER'S QUESTION

13. **"What do you know about this company?"**
Select the strongest answer.

(A) I've done research on the company and checked out the mission statement and what you stand for. I am very familiar with your products and the companies you are competing against. I looked up the backgrounds of your two founders and traced their careers and successes. I know that your current stock price is down but that you have a new product in the wings. I know you are a company that I am very interested in joining.

(B) My interest in this company began when I was in college and did a research paper on companies and stocks. I have followed the progress of the company: the ups and the downs. I know that there are currently some deals in the works that may change the makeup of the company as well as its standing in the industry. I have targeted this company as the place where I want to spend my career.

(C) When I found the posting on the Internet, I wasn't really familiar with the company. I began asking friends and colleagues what they knew about the company. They all had really positive things to say about working for this company. I have heard that this company really treats its employees well and that the benefits here are top of the line.

ANSWERS
The Strongest Answer

(A) This is the strongest answer because of the skills demonstrated: not only researching the company but digging deeper for information about the founders, the competition, future products, and stock. This answer provides information and knowledge beyond what was on the website.

The Mediocre Answer

(B) This is not a bad answer. There is enthusiasm for the company and a history of research. The answer lacks information on what is happening in the company, the competition, and the company's standing in the industry. All that information can be found by searching on-line or at the public library.

The Weakest Answer

(C) This is the weakest answer because it does not provide any facts to talk about. Unfortunately, it's not unusual for candidates to lack information about the company. At the very least a visit to the company website is essential. Relying on the "word" from friends and colleagues is not as good as doing research. This answer also focuses on "the benefits" of working for the company, not on the company itself.

RATE YOURSELF

If you chose answer **(A)**, give yourself 5 points.

If you chose answer **(B)**, give yourself 3 points.

If you chose answer **(C)**, give yourself 0 points.   _____

The Internet is an excellent source of information on any company. Give yourself a competitive edge by doing your "homework" and researching the company before taking the interview.

INTERVIEWER'S QUESTION

14. "What do you think are the key qualities for a support person?"
Select the strongest answer.

(A) Communication skills are the most critical. A good support person deals with a number of executives and key customers. Communications skills are extremely important. I have had to plan many social events and conferences where my communication skills were important to the success of the project. My bosses have depended heavily on my communication skills to convey messages and explain sensitive situations when necessary.

(B) It really depends on the nature of the job and the responsibilities involved. I sometimes support groups and at other times work with individual bosses. Whatever I do, I try to accommodate each person as well as I can. If I am working for an individual, I work as a "right-hand man." I have been able to support the people I have worked for by staying flexible and trying to satisfy the requirements presented to me.

(C) Some of the key skills needed are being organized, having good communication skills, being flexible, being reliable, and being a team player. These particular skills are some of the skills I pride myself on having. I have excellent communication skills and respond well when asked to work on projects that are not part of my everyday job. I respond quickly and never miss deadlines. My teammates would tell you that if I don't have something to do, I ask others if I can be of help.

ANSWERS

The Strongest Answer

(C) This is the strongest answer because it names the key qualities and then takes the opportunity to point out that you have them. By talking about your key skills this answer becomes stronger, especially with the "teammate" endorsement.

The Mediocre Answer

(A) This is not a bad answer, but it focuses on only one quality instead of naming the "key qualities." The answer gives good examples of communication skills and how you have used the skill in your past work. It would be stronger if you had answered the question as asked. Be sure you are listening to—and answering—the questions asked.

The Weakest Answer

(B) This is the weakest answer because it lacks the focus to convey what the key qualities are and whether you have them. By giving a "neutral" answer you fail to make an impact. In this case the question did not ask about "your" key qualities but about what you thought the key qualities were. It is all right to say that you have the qualities needed as long as you answer the question at the same time.

RATE YOURSELF

If you chose answer (C), give yourself 5 points.

If you chose answer (A), give yourself 3 points.

If you chose answer (B), give yourself 0 points.   _____

INTERVIEWER'S QUESTION

15. **"Describe your leadership or management style."**
Select the strongest answer.

(A) I am very "bottom-line-driven." The customer is the most important product and the one who makes it possible to pay the bills. It's a numbers game. The more customers you have, the more revenue is generated. I believe in customer service. I believe in empowering my team to do whatever it takes to satisfy the customer. I believe that if you have a solid customer base, you have a profitable business.

(B) I lead by example. I work hard and meet deadlines, and I expect my subordinates to do the same thing. I don't mind assisting when there are problems, but I don't believe in holding anyone's hand through projects. I assign the work and expect that the work will get done. If I have to look over shoulders to keep people on schedule, I am not a good manager. My preferred style in a boss is the "hands-off" approach. Just give me an assignment and let me go to work.

(C) If you asked my team members, they would tell you that I am a fair and open manager. I make myself available every day. My objective is to recognize people for their strengths. I recently promoted a team member who had begun as a problem employee but through some one-on-one coaching from me, along with his willingness to put in some extra time, became a star.

ANSWERS

The Strongest Answer

(C) This is strongest answer because it gives a specific example and an indirect endorsement from your team. These are good techniques to use when you are answering a subjective question like this one. It also demonstrates a genuine commitment to the team members and to letting them know that their work counts in the bigger picture and provides a specific example of how you do that.

The Mediocre Answer

(A) This answer does not show a basic understanding of leadership. It certainly addresses where the management focus is: "making money through customers." However, it does not address the internal customer: the worker. It talks about empowering people, which is positive.

The Weakest Answer

(B) Depending on how the position description is written and what they are looking for, this answer shows a very hands-off approach to management. "Give them the work and let them struggle" is the message here. Most companies prefer managers who work with and develop their people.

RATE YOURSELF

If you chose answer **(C)**, give yourself 5 points.

If you chose answer **(A)**, give yourself 3 points.

If you chose answer **(B)**, give yourself 0 points.   _____

INTERVIEWER'S QUESTION

16. **"In what ways has your current or last job prepared you to take on more responsibility?"**
Select the strongest answer.

(A) I had extensive experience working with customers in my last job. In the beginning I had to learn to deal with people who were very frustrated and wanted to take their feelings out on me. I have to admit that in the beginning it really would get to me when someone was being nasty and rude. Since that time, I've taken some training courses on selling and human behavior that have helped immensely. I needed that experience to be able to move forward to a job like this one.

(B) My current job is really not a good fit for me. I am overqualified and somewhat bored. I took the job knowing that I could do it without much of a stretch. The job before this one was a real "burnout" type of environment, and I needed a job that was kind of low-key. I am now ready to move forward and give my all to this job. I know I could do this job and bring added value to the department.

(C) My last job was a great stepping-stone for me to take on the new challenges this job will provide. I had to deal with all kinds of situations and people in my last job. After five years in that job I am ready for some new challenges in a new industry. I know I am ready to move up and would be good at this job because I have the patience needed to deal with difficult people.

ANSWERS

The Strongest Answer

(A) This is the strongest answer because it clearly gives an example of growth and experience. It also talks about training and development to get an understanding beyond the job itself. This is a good example of showing how your past experience is an indicator of your future success.

The Mediocre Answer

(C) This is not a bad answer, but it focuses on "what's in it for me." Most people want "new challenges" in the next job. When too much focus is on the challenge, it takes away from what you bring to the job. The bottom line to the interview process is "What can you bring to this company?"

The Weakest Answer

(B) This answer has all the indicators of a person who suffered from "burnout" and took any job just to survive. The interviewer might have reason to be concerned that this will happen again. It is best not to talk about the negatives of any job. Put the focus on the experience and skills you can bring to the new position: "I can bring added value to the job because of my past experience working in fast-paced environments."

RATE YOURSELF

If you chose answer **(A)**, give yourself 5 points.

If you chose answer **(C)**, give yourself 3 points.

If you chose answer **(B)**, give yourself 0 points.   _____

INTERVIEWER'S QUESTION

17. **"What do you value most in a teammate?"**
    Select the strongest answer.

    (A) I've worked with a wide variety of people, and the ones who are of most value to me are those who are dependable. One of my pet peeves is to hand off something and find out that it was never taken care of. I don't understand how some people keep their jobs when they can't be depended on to complete the job.

    (B) I really value teammates who are supportive and are willing to do whatever it takes. One project at my last company really put my team to the test when one of the members had an accident and had to take time off. Even though we each had our own deadlines, we all jumped in to fill the gap when it occurred. It meant two additional long weekends, but we had a common goal. We were able to meet the deadline and feel good about helping someone with a problem.

    (C) I value communication skills in any work I do, but in particular when I work with teams. I think it is essential for everyone on the team to be able to express himself or herself in a clear manner and be able to listen and follow directions. When communications break down, there is no team. Language skills are the most important part of any team effort.

ANSWERS
The Strongest Answer

(B) This is the strongest answer because it gives a clear example that backs up your opinion. The answer is secondary to the message it conveys. Teamwork means getting along and working together.

The Mediocre Answer

(A) This answer could be viewed as complaining or negative. Being dependable is an important trait, but the answer would be stronger if it were phrased in a more positive manner: "I value dependability from teammates because it means the work gets completed and everyone benefits."

The Weakest Answer

(C) This answer takes on a life of its own and goes down a different path. The answer deals more with effective communication than with "the value of a teammate." The answer is not a wrong answer—communication skills are very desirable. It just doesn't relate to the question being asked.

RATE YOURSELF

If you chose answer **(B)**, give yourself 5 points.

If you chose answer **(A)**, give yourself 3 points.

If you chose answer **(C)**, give yourself 0 points.   _____

INTERVIEWER'S QUESTION

18. **"What are the most important things for you in any job/company?"**
    Select the strongest answer.

    (A) I look for a company that is growth-oriented, a place that is secure, where I can grow with the company. There are so many changes going on in the industry that I am seeking a company that has a solid reputation and foundation. I look for jobs where there has been low turnover because that usually is an indicator of the way people are treated and the benefits they are given.

    (B) The number one thing that I look for in a job is the opportunity it allows. To have a chance to work on something really interesting that might make a difference in people's personal or professional lives is my idea of job satisfaction. I don't mean that I want to save the world, but if I can contribute to a company and the goal of that company, I know I can find satisfaction.

    (C) The first thing I look for is job satisfaction. What I mean by that is a feeling that my work is of importance in some way to the bottom line or the bigger scheme of things. I also look for jobs that have advancement opportunities. I want to grow with the company. Lastly, I would like to enjoy my coworkers and have some fun. I spend a lot of time at my job and want it to be a good experience.

ANSWERS

The Strongest Answer

(C) This is the strongest answer because it offers a broader sweep of values than the others do. Job satisfaction is among the top values of most candidates. Because you explain what job satisfaction means to you, the interviewer has a better idea of your career interests. Read through the job ad and determine what values are important at this company. If your values are in line with the company's values, this is an opportunity to let the interviewer know that you will "fit in" and enjoy working there.

The Mediocre Answer

(B) This is not a bad answer, but it may come across as a bit too ideal or "canned." It's like answering that you want world peace. It is a good idea to be interested in the company's bigger picture and to be a part of that picture, but you would sound better rounded and more realistic if you mentioned a few values that were broader-based, such as teamwork, authenticity, balance, or the need for a challenge.

The Weakest Answer

(A) This is the weakest answer because it is focused too much on your benefits. This answer might be seen as an indicator of your insecurity, presenting you as someone looking for security in a company. No company can guarantee security in today's world of change; that is an unrealistic goal. Asking about turnover is a good idea, but don't state it as one of your criteria in an interview.

RATE YOURSELF

If you chose answer (C), give yourself 5 points.

If you chose answer (B), give yourself 3 points.

If you chose answer (A), give yourself 0 points.   _____

Job ads/postings are gifts given to you by the employer. This is a wish list of qualities for the job. If you do a comparison between what they are looking for and what you want in a job, you will have an idea whether this is a good match for you. If the job is not a good match, you might want to reconsider applying for it. Would you really want this job?

INTERVIEWER'S QUESTION

19. **"How do you stay current and informed about industry trends and technology?"**

Select the strongest answer.

(A) I do all the standard things. I read the business section of the newspaper daily. I research the Internet for information on the industry. I attend a local networking organization and subscribe to an industry journal. I belong to a professional organization and attend monthly meetings to network and stay in touch. I really like what I do, and so it is interesting to me to learn and keep current with the ever-changing world we live in.

(B) I use the Internet and check the news sites to see what is happening in the world. I don't get around to the newspaper, but I do subscribe to a weekly news magazine that keeps me up to date fairly well. I feel that I am more informed than the average person.

(C) There isn't much time left in the day after my long work hours. I have been working overtime for the past year. My busy life does not allow for much more than watching the evening news to catch up with the latest happenings. I always read my company's newsletters and the bulletins it sends out to keep in touch with what's happening in the company.

ANSWERS

The Strongest Answer

(A) This answer has a very natural, relaxed tone to it, yet it covers every possible base and states that you are a person who is "out there" and informed. By being involved in groups and organizations you also are widening your network, which is the number one way to get a job. Of course, in your interview you'd give the specific names of newsletters and organizations.

The Mediocre Answer

(B) This answer is not a bad one; it just limits your information by the sources you use to stay informed. You are correct that you are probably more informed than the average person, but you are competing to be above-average in the interview process. Often a company is seeking someone who is connected to the industry and looks at the groups to which you belong.

The Weakest Answer

(C) Although this might be a "real" answer, this is not the strongest position to be in as an informed person. Regardless of the position you hold in a company, staying informed about the latest trends and issues is crucial for job success.

RATE YOURSELF

If you chose answer (A), give yourself 5 points.

If you chose answer (B), give yourself 3 points.

If you chose answer (C), give yourself 0 points.   _____

INTERVIEWER'S QUESTION

20. **"Do you believe you're overqualified for this position?"**
Select the strongest answer.

(A) Are you concerned about my ability to succeed in this position? I can assure you that I always work hard and get my work done no matter what my title or my salary. My work is very important to me, and I want to make a difference. When you talk about being overqualified, I'm not sure what that means. If you think my salary is too high, I can assure you that the opportunity is far more important than the pay. I want this job, and if you choose me, I will prove I can do the job, bringing my experience and successes with me.

(B) From the first time I read the ad for this position, I knew that I could do the job and do it well. I have extensive experience that will enhance the position as described, bringing new ideas and methods. I have a record of proven success in bringing order to chaos and making things run more efficiently. From what we've been talking about today, I feel I could be the solution to your problem. I wouldn't call that overqualified. I'd call it a good deal.

(C) That would depend on your definition of overqualified. I have been in this industry a long time. I remember when we did things without computers. I have learned the hard way, not just from taking classes like these young kids do, but through hard work and trial and error. I have a great work ethic, and anyone who has ever worked for me would tell you I'm a dedicated person who is very reliable. I always meet the deadlines and goals that I set for myself. I was taught that you earn your pay, not just collect it by showing up.

ANSWERS

The Strongest Answer

(B) This is the strongest answer because it sounds upbeat and per-
suasive. You can bring something that the new company needs,
and you can provide added value. One of the concerns when
someone is overqualified is that he or she won't stick around.
That concern could be addressed in subsequent answers.

The Mediocre Answer

(A) The answer isn't bad; it just has a tone of desperation, almost like
begging for the job. This should be a situation that is win-win for
everyone: "Here's what I have to offer. What are you looking
for?" One of the concerns about someone who has many years of
experience is that the salary requirement will be too high.
Nevertheless, it is best not to bring up this subject until the interviewer asks about it.

The Weakest Answer

(C) This answer sounds dusty and needs to be refreshed. When
someone thinks you are overqualified, he or she may relate that
to your years of experience. One of the things the interviewer
may be concerned with is your ability to be cutting-edge. When
you talk about not having computers in the "good old days,"
interviewers begin to think their suspicions are correct.

RATE YOURSELF

If you chose answer (B), give yourself 5 points.

If you chose answer (A), give yourself 3 points.

If you chose answer (C), give yourself 0 points.   _____

Vocabulary is very important in interviewing. Don't make yourself
appear older by saying things like "young kids" or quoting old say-
ings. Using appropriate language could be the difference between
success and failure. Check several job postings for current language
used in the company or industry.

INTERVIEWER'S QUESTION

21. **"If I asked your coworkers to say three positive things about you, what would they say?"**
Select the strongest answer.

(A) They probably would tell you that I am very knowledgeable about my job and am willing to share my knowledge with them whenever they need help. Second, they would tell you that I have great organizational skills. I plan ahead and meet schedules. The third thing they would tell you is that I know when to laugh. I've learned through experience that you can't take situations too seriously.

(B) I'm not really sure what they would say. We all work well together but don't have much social interaction. I think they would tell you that I am a hard worker, because I am. I think they would tell you I am a very thoughtful person; at least I try to be. And I think they would say I am a team player. I always try to help others.

(C) That's a difficult question. I think they think I am responsible. I'm always cooperative. I don't gossip or get involved in company politics. On the negative side, some of them think I'm aloof because I don't get involved in the gossip. But I think it is best to keep work on a nonpersonal basis.

ANSWERS
The Strongest Answer

(A) This is the strongest answer not only because of the examples but because the skills named are a mixture of skills. You gave an example of your work knowledge; your organizational skills, which can be applied in any job; and your personal traits, which make you a likable person. It's best when you can give a mixture of skills and traits. That is what makes you unique.

The Mediocre Answer

(B) This answer would be stronger if you gave some reasons for the answers, such as, "They would tell you I am a very thoughtful person. I always remember everyone's birthday and send a card or a little gift." When you give an example with the statement, it makes more of an impact. Also, avoid the phrase "I think." It makes you appear less confident.

The Weakest Answer

(C) This answer is weak because it does not have a positive viewpoint and turns negative at the end. Never volunteer a negative thought about yourself unless you are asked for a weakness. This answer does not give the impression that you are much of a team player.

RATE YOURSELF

If you chose answer **(A)**, give yourself 5 points.

If you chose answer **(B)**, give yourself 3 points.

If you chose answer **(C)**, give yourself 0 points.   _____

INTERVIEWER'S QUESTION

22. **"Why should we hire you?"**
    Select the strongest answer.

    (A) I can do this job. I know I can. Because I am a quick learner, I have the ability to pick up things faster than most people can. I currently am taking classes to learn some of the computer programs I don't know. I can learn this job very fast and be useful almost immediately. I am looking for an opportunity to try something new.

    (B) My strong people skills are what I can bring to this job and company. I have an ability to read people and treat them as individuals in a way that most people can't. My customers always ask for me personally because they know I will give them excellent service. When I saw this job posted on the Internet, I knew that this was "my" job.

    (C) If you compare my qualifications with your requirements, you will see that I am almost a perfect match for this position. You are seeking someone with the years of experience and skills I have acquired in this industry, and in addition to that I have excellent writing skills. I have the ability to work with a wide variety of people at all levels. If you were to ask my former colleagues, they would tell you, "She is one of a kind. She keeps the morale up and the work flowing."

ANSWERS

The Strongest Answer

(C) This is the strongest answer. The best way to persuade the interviewer that you are the best person for the job is to present yourself as being as close a match to the requirements as possible. Let them know that you are a match by telling them about your skills, particularly in the specific areas required. If you have something additional to bring to the job, that will make a difference; it may be the deciding factor in whether you get the offer. Quoting colleagues or bosses helps prove your point without your having to say so.

The Mediocre Answer

(B) This is not as strong an answer (C), but it has the right tone. Consider stating one or two strong points that you have outside the job description: an "added value." This answer also shows strong confidence in yourself and your ability to do the job.

The Weakest Answer

(A) This is the weakest answer because it has a desperate tone. It's a difficult sell when you do not have the requirements for the job. This answer does demonstrate an eager attitude and a proven ability to learn quickly, which is the right approach to take when you are lacking skills. Remember that the company is not in business to teach you new things but to get the work done.

RATE YOURSELF

If you chose answer (C), give yourself 5 points.

If you chose answer (B), give yourself 3 points.

If you chose answer (A), give yourself 0 points.   _____

INTERVIEWER'S QUESTION

23. **"If I remember only one thing about you, what should that be?"**
Select the strongest answer.

   (A) I have an unusual hobby that you might remember my mentioning. I collect one-of-a-kind stamps that have printing errors. I have a collection worth thousands of dollars.

   (B) I can be remembered for my excellent communication skills and experience working with all types of people. I really want to help people.

   (C) I have two skills that are distinctly different but that define my personality. I am a very good pianist and an excellent computer "guy." I'm known for my love of keyboards.

ANSWERS

The Strongest Answer

(C) This is the strongest answer, especially if computer skills are needed for the job. Obviously, you will not always be able to relate your hobbies to your job, but you can see how this would make the interviewer remember you after you finished the interview. The idea is to find something that sets you apart from everyone else.

The Mediocre Answer

(A) This is a very interesting answer that would qualify as a "memorable" statement, but it's not as strong as answer (C) because it doesn't relate directly to the job. If you could somehow tie your hobby into the job functions, your answer would be stronger. For instance, you might say, "I have a valuable stamp collection that is rare because I only collect stamps with errors. I started doing this because of my strong attention to detail and ability to pick up on errors. It became a challenge." You've given a skill—"attention to detail"–that is relevant to most jobs.

The Weakest Answer

(B) The problem with this answer is that it is one that a lot of other people could give. There is nothing unique about it. The idea of being good with people and communications is good, but you will need to expand on the idea to make it stand out: "Because of my excellent communication skills I am able to break down complex problems into user-friendly concepts. I'm known as 'the word wizard' at my current company."

RATE YOURSELF

If you chose answer (C), give yourself 5 points.

If you chose answer (A), give yourself 3 points.

If you chose answer (B), give yourself 0 points.   _____

INTERVIEWER'S QUESTION

24. **"What are your salary expectations?"**
    Select the strongest answer.

    (A) My current salary is $50,000. I also have stock options and bonuses and a very generous benefits package. I would like to compare your benefits package before I give you an exact number.

    (B) I really need more information about the job and other benefits before I can come up with a figure. I think after I have the facts we can come to a mutually agreeable figure. Could you share with me the range that you have budgeted for the position?

    (C) I'm sure whatever you offer will be a fair amount for a person with my experience and qualifications. I am more interested in working for this company and the opportunity that it allows.

ANSWERS

The Strongest Answer

(B) This is the stronger answer because it postpones the conversation until there are more facts available. It also puts the onus on the employer by asking what range has been budgeted. Until you have a thorough understanding of the job responsibilities and the range allowed for a person with your background or experience, you cannot give the interviewer an accurate figure.

The Mediocre Answer

(C) This is a nice way of saying, "I trust you to treat me fairly," which could be viewed as somewhat passive. When the time comes, you can push harder for what you want. Be sure you know what the "going rate" is for someone with your experience and qualifications in your area by checking some salary websites. You can find current ones by doing a search for "salary" on your favorite search engine.

The Weakest Answer

(A) There is an interviewing rule that states, "Never give out a number first. The person who mentions a figure first loses." When you give a number such as $50,000, you are taking a chance because it may be too high for this position or possibly too low. It is best to get the interviewer to name the number by asking for the "range allowed."

RATE YOURSELF

If you chose answer **(B)**, give yourself 5 points.

If you chose answer **(C)**, give yourself 3 points.

If you chose answer **(A)**, give yourself 0 points.   _____

INTERVIEWER'S QUESTION

25. **"Do you have any questions?"**
    Select the strongest answer.

    (A) I would like to know about the bonus situation and how it is decided who will receive a bonus and who will not. I also would like to know more about payment of the premiums on health-care insurance.

    (B) You have been very thorough in your explanation of what the job entails. I don't have any further questions at this time. I'm sure I would have more questions once I started the job.

    (C) One thing that has been talked about during the interview process is the "branding" of your product. Could you tell me what has worked to this point and what you would expect to see done differently?

ANSWERS

The Strongest Answer

(C) This is the strongest answer because it shows that you have been listening and are aware that one of your first projects will be to work on the "branding" issue. The bottom line of the interviewing process is "What can you do for us?" By asking what has worked and what has not, you demonstrate an ability to listen to the problem, and then you can address what is needed to solve the problem.

The Mediocre Answer

(A) Depending on where you are in the interview process, this answer could be appropriate. This would not be a good question to ask in a first interview before any interest is shown. This question focuses on what you will get out of working for this company. You will need the information eventually; just wait until the appropriate time to bring it up, such as during a second interview or after an offer has been made.

The Weakest Answer

(B) This is the most common reply used by candidates—"No, I don't have any questions"—and it is the wrong answer. It is very important that you ask questions to show your interest and let the interviewer know you have been listening.

RATE YOURSELF

If you chose answer (C), give yourself 5 points.

If you chose answer (A), give yourself 3 points.

If you chose answer (B), give yourself 0 points.   _____

The best questions come from what is heard during the interview. Pay attention to the questions asked during the interview. You can pick up valuable information by listening to what is said and what is not said. Read between the lines and then ask for more information.

Behavioral Interview Questions

This section of the Interview IQ Test focuses on behavioral interview questions. As we've discussed, these types of questions are being used more frequently by all kinds of companies because they allow the interviewer to find out what specific skills, knowledge, and experience the job candidate possesses. Behavioral interview questions can be recognized by the wording used. A typical behavioral question might start with one of the following: "Tell me about ..."

"Can you give me an example?"

"Describe a time ..."

"What was the biggest/most important/most difficult ...?"

"When was the ...?"

As soon as you hear the interviewer asking for an example, you will know that an example story of your work experience is being sought as proof that you actually have the background you claim to have on your résumé and that is required for the job. The key to answering behavioral questions is to be *specific*. The more recent and job-related the example is, the more effective your answer will be.

If you do not have a recent, work-related example to relay, use a volunteer, college, or life experience. The important point is that it in some way relate to the qualities sought for the job for which you are applying.

In Part 2 you will learn how to write and tell your own stories in an organized, succinct manner, relaying your experiences and showing the interviewer that you have had successes and could repeat those successes at the new company.

Turn the page for the behavioral section of the Interview IQ Test.

INTERVIEWER'S QUESTION

26. **"Tell me about the biggest project you've worked on from start to finish."**
    Select the strongest answer.

    (A) The company I worked for received a huge order; in fact, it was the biggest order the company ever achieved. The order was for a major client, and the completion of the order would be a major bonus for us and a revenue stream for the future. Our challenge was a pricing issue. To design what we set out to design became unreasonable because of the cost of materials and labor. After many meetings we were able to combine some of the features of the product and still satisfy the customer. I never worked harder on a project to meet an unrealistic expectation.

    (B) We had a safety project that most of us had had little or no experience with before. We really had to pull together and share information and resources to pull this one off. Fortunately, we all got along well and supported one another. We were able to put together this project with a lot of effort. We stayed late and worked weekends for two months. We worked closely with the other departments in the company to make sure we were meeting the customers' needs. The good news is that we were able to get it done. Everybody felt really good about pulling together on this one.

    (C) I was in charge of designing the safety program for a huge order received by my last company. The first thing I did was to select three top technicians to work with me. We worked as a team, with each of us assigned a piece of the project. I led the group by coordinating the schedules and making sure all the deadlines were met. I was in constant communication with my team members and was there to troubleshoot as needed. Because of the open communication between the four of us, we were able to complete the project ahead of the shipping date.

ANSWERS

The Strongest Answer

(C) This is the strongest answer because it gives a very clear picture, with details of the situation. Even though this was a team situation, the interviewer is able to see "your" role in solving the problem. By using the pronoun "I" you give a clearer picture of the skills you used. This example talks about some of the skills you used: leadership, coordinating, follow-through, tracking, communication, problem solving, time management, and troubleshooting.

The Mediocre Answer

(B) There is a definite problem with this answer: There are too many "we"s (seven to be exact) and not enough "I"s (none). The interviewer has no idea what "your" role was. While it is important to give credit where credit is due, it is also necessary to describe what you did to pull this project together as a team member or leader.

The Weakest Answer

(A) This is a weak answer because it puts too much emphasis on the company and the project and not enough on "your" role. What exactly was your role in this team effort? One of the biggest mistakes candidates make is not saying what their role was. More details of your actions are needed for this to be a strong answer.

RATE YOURSELF

If you chose answer **(C)**, give yourself 5 points.

If you chose answer **(B)**, give yourself 3 points.

If you chose answer **(A)**, give yourself 0 points.   _____

The correct use of the pronouns "I" and "we" in your stories is critical. While it is important to not take credit for something that the team did, it is equally important to give yourself credit for your role in a project. When you use "we" instead of "I," it is difficult for the interviewer to determine your role.

INTERVIEWER'S QUESTION

27. **"Tell me about a time when you had to overcome obstacles to get your job done."**
Select the strongest answer.

(A) When I was a project manager for an entertainment company, I had to coordinate the video presentation for a very important meeting with an extremely tight deadline. The problem was that not all the film arrived. The first thing I did was get in touch with the other branches to see if anyone else had copies of the film. I was able to find everything I needed and have it shipped overnight. I stayed until three in the morning to get the project done, but it was quality work and was completed on time. My boss gave me extra points for getting through that one.

(B) I have to work around obstacles all the time. It's the nature of the job of managing projects. One day I have to work around money issues; the next day it's schedules and deadlines. Of course I always have people problems to contend with. Every day I plan my day, and then, right when I am getting ahead, some problem occurs. Fortunately, I am known for my problem-solving ability.

(C) I have had many times in my jobs when I have had to put in extra time to solve some problem or obstacle that came up. One thing I always do is try to think logically and stay focused. I usually can work through anything that comes my way. I have had times when a whole project depended on me to get it out the door on time. I came through with flying colors. My boss is sometimes amazed at what I can accomplish.

ANSWERS

The Strongest Answer

(A) This is the only answer of the three that addresses the question asked. The question begins, "Tell me about a time." Whenever you are asked about "a time," the interviewer is looking for a specific example. This answer shows that you handled the crisis, how you did it, and the result of your efforts.

The Mediocre Answer

(C) This is not a bad answer, but it doesn't answer the question. It is very general and needs to be more specific. A lot of good qualities can be heard in this answer, but there is no specific example. Anyone can say he or she stays cool under pressure, but the interviewer is looking for an example of when you actually did that.

The Weakest Answer

(B) This answer is very nonspecific. It is very general and does not provide an example of "a time when" you had to overcome an obstacle. It would be a much stronger answer if it included specific details of how and when you solved a problem. The tone of this answer could also be a problem. An interviewer might read between the lines and pick up on the idea that you are "burned-out" on this work.

RATE YOURSELF

If you chose answer **(A)**, give yourself 5 points.

If you chose answer **(C)**, give yourself 3 points.

If you chose answer **(B)**, give yourself 0 points.   _____

INTERVIEWER'S QUESTION

28. **"Tell me about a time when you had to handle a stressful situation."**
Select the strongest answer.

(A) That's the way of life in this profession. We always seem to be short-staffed. If you can't handle the stress, you can't succeed as a nurse. We all work as hard as we can and as fast as we can; but sometimes that's just not enough. We get complaints and have to deal with it. I have had instances where I have had as many as 20 patients and had to handle it. That's just the nature of the game. I'm good at what I do, and I do with whatever it takes. There are always shortages and budget problems, and you just have to deal with it. I have what is needed to do the job.

(B) We were short-staffed because two nurses called in sick. I and another nurse were the only ones on duty, and we had 28 patients to care for. It was one of those times when everything that could go wrong did: Patients were yelling, and one patient fell. The other nurse and I discussed the situation and did a quick priority check. By partnering we kept cool and supported each other rather than criticizing and stressing. We would give each other a little smile or a hand signal from time to time to let the other one know that we were hanging in there. Somehow we got through the night and assisted every patient, but at the time it was very stressful.

(C) I know what it takes to get this job done. I pride myself on staying calm when everything around me is falling apart. I don't like stress, but I know how to deal with it. I just do my work and try to ignore the unpleasant things that take place. I'm paid to do a service, and I do it. We each have our own area of responsibility. I do mine, and I do it well. I get through my shift, and that's the end. I don't take problems home with me.

ANSWERS

The Strongest Answer

(B) This is the strongest answer because it provides an example of a real team player handling stressful situations. This reply demonstrates by example the ability to remain cool and think straight when things are too hot to handle. The skills heard in this example are teamwork, adaptability, the ability to handle pressure, the ability to prioritize, a sense of humor, and the ability to communicate.

The Mediocre Answer

(A) This is not the strongest answer, but it does have merit. It does not give a specific example as was asked for in the question. It would be a stronger answer if it was expanded with a specific example. The statement "I've had as many as 20 patients" shows the scope of responsibility; but a specific example would have shown the skills it took to deal with the situation.

The Weakest Answer

(C) This is the weakest answer. In addition to sounding negative, it does not address the question about a specific time. This answer has the tone of someone with a defeatist attitude. That may be the way things are, but the answer points out all the negatives of the job and none of the positives. This answer could be interpreted as coming from a person who is burned-out or has given up trying to improve the situation.

RATE YOURSELF

If you chose answer **(B)**, give yourself 5 points.

If you chose answer **(A)**, give yourself 3 points.

If you chose answer **(C)**, give yourself 0 points.   _____

INTERVIEWER'S QUESTION

29. **"Your résumé states that you're a 'hard worker.' Can you give me an example of a time when you worked hard?"**

    Select the strongest answer.

    (A) I always try to get the work done on time. Sometimes that means working overtime. Sometimes I can't get all my work done during the day and am willing to stay late to finish up. There have been times when I just couldn't get everything done no matter how hard I worked. I always do my best to meet deadlines, but sometimes you just have to let go. I'd rather do it right and be late than do it wrong and be on time.

    (B) I am a very hard worker. I am always punctual and get my work done. The tighter the deadline is, the harder I work. I plan my day so that I'm never late with my work, and I always meet deadlines. If you asked my last boss, he would tell you what a hard worker I am. I do whatever I have to do to get the job done.

    (C) My boss had a really important project, and it didn't look like we were going to make the deadline. I volunteered to do some late nights and weekends. My boss and two other coworkers worked seven straight days with no time off. My piece of the project was to coordinate all the information and enter the data. It was a real team effort, but we were able to meet the deadline, and that made my boss look good. He rewarded us all for our efforts.

ANSWERS

The Strongest Answer

(C) This is the strongest answer because it gives a specific example of going "above and beyond" what was expected. Some of the skills that appear in this answer are initiative, teamwork, coordination skills, a great attitude, and a cooperative spirit—and a willingness to make the boss look good.

The Mediocre Answer

(B) This is not as strong an answer. It provides all the right traits—punctual, conscientious, good attitude—but no examples of using those traits in an actual situation. This answer does benefit from the endorsement from your boss. Bringing the boss into the story is a great way to strengthen the story.

The Weakest Answer

(A) This is the weakest answer because it does not include an example of working hard and emphasizes meeting deadlines, which is not quite the same skill. The interviewer could get the idea that you miss deadlines and have a difficult time keeping up with the workload. This answer needs to emphasize the times you stayed late and why the workload was too big to handle.

RATE YOURSELF

If you chose answer **(C)**, give yourself 5 points.

If you chose answer **(B)**, give yourself 3 points.

If you chose answer **(A)**, give yourself 0 points.   _____

INTERVIEWER'S QUESTION

30. **"Tell me about a time when you had a disagreement or confrontation with a boss or coworker."**
    Select the strongest answer.

   (A) My boss refused to take action against an employee who was getting away with something that went against company policy. I was upset about the situation. I feel that everyone should be treated equally and that it was wrong for this person to get away with something when the rest of us had to conform. I talked to my boss, but that didn't work. I ended up going to human resources and complaining. My boss was unhappy with me for going over his head, but action was taken and the employee was disciplined. My boss eventually got over it.

   (B) I'm one of those people who try to get along with everyone. I try to ignore people who have irritating qualities. It's just not worth getting into a snit about that. I try to be as professional as possible when I work. If I get upset, I go for a walk or take a break to get away from the situation. I really don't like confrontation.

   (C) There was a coworker who was taking extra time off at lunch and giving me a problem because I was her backup. Rather than let it fester, I asked her if we could talk after work. I explained to her in a nonaccusing manner that there was a problem. She told me that she had been trying to accomplish personal tasks at lunch that were taking longer than expected and that she would stop doing that. She hadn't thought about the impact it was having on my work. Things changed for the better after our discussion.

ANSWERS

The Strongest Answer

(C) This is the strongest answer. Communication skills are the most important skills in most jobs. This answer demonstrates an ability to face up to difficult situations and "nip the problem" before it becomes full-blown.

The Mediocre Answer

(A) This is a good answer because it is specific, but it is a bit risky to give an example of a time when you went against your boss. This incident had a positive result, but if you were interviewing with a hiring manager, it might cause some doubt about your cooperativeness as an employee. It would be advisable to stay away from stories that make your boss look weak, especially if you are interviewing with your "future" boss.

The Weakest Answer

(B) This isn't a bad answer, but it is somewhat passive, as seen in the phrases "I try to ignore people," "If I get upset, I go for a walk," and "I really don't like confrontation." What an interviewer might hear is that you are a person who "stuffs" things and holds them in rather than taking any action. Some employees who are passive have a breaking point when they reach their limit and "boil over"; they are known as "passive-aggressive." It's all right to be irritated by fellow employees. The issue becomes how you handle the situation—your communication and judgment skills.

RATE YOURSELF

If you chose answer **(C)**, give yourself 5 points.

If you chose answer **(A)**, give yourself 3 points.

If you chose answer **(B)**, give yourself 0 points.   _____

INTERVIEWER'S QUESTION

31. **"What was the most difficult problem you've handled? How did you deal with it?"**

Select the strongest answer.

(A) I work hard every day. I have a high work ethic for myself and always do my job and more. My boss would tell you that I am a really dedicated worker. One of my strengths is my ability to see a problem through to the end no matter what it takes. I have been known to stay until 10 or 11 at night to see a project through to completion. I get a lot of satisfaction when I see a job through.

(B) It was our peak season, and we were behind schedule. We only had two weeks left before the deadline. I stepped up to the plate and gathered the team leaders to talk about the situation. We brainstormed some ideas about how we could meet the customer's deadline. One of my ideas was to divide the project into specific pieces, which isn't the way it was done before. Each person was in charge of a section. I made sure everyone stayed on track by checking with all of them every evening before the close of business. It was a remarkable effort, but we were able to come in under deadline.

(C) I guess everyone would define hard work differently. Hard work is getting the job done and doing it right the first time. I get irritated when someone on the team is not pulling his or her weight. I strongly believe that we are all accountable to ourselves and shouldn't have to have a manager looking over our shoulders to get our work done. I was raised with the ethic of "Work hard to earn your salary, and you will get what you deserve in return."

ANSWERS
The Strongest Answer

    (B) This answer demonstrates several skills: leadership, creative thinking, problem solving, follow-through, and being a team player. When the question is answered with a specific example, the interviewer can hear the strong skills demonstrated. Patterns begin to develop, and a picture of the way you work is formed.

The Mediocre Answer

    (A) The words are there; the example is not. Saying that you can go "above and beyond" is stronger when you can describe a time when you did that. This answer brings in a third party—the boss—which strengthens the statement, "I am a hard worker; my boss would tell you that," but it provides no example that substantiates that statement.

The Weakest Answer

    (C) This is the weakest answer because it "preaches." The question was not about defining what hard work is. It asked for an example. You have on your résumé "hard worker." The interviewer wants to know what you think you did that was hard work.

RATE YOURSELF

If you chose answer **(B)**, give yourself 5 points.

If you chose answer **(A)**, give yourself 3 points.

If you chose answer **(C)**, give yourself 0 points.   _____

A good rule to follow is to *never* put anything on your résumé or say something in an interview that you cannot back up with a story. If you state it, you should be able to prove it with an example.

INTERVIEWER'S QUESTION

32. **"Tell me about a time when you had to adapt quickly to a change."**
    Select the strongest answer.

    (A) When I ran the numbers on a certain food item, I discovered that sales were declining. I had to move quickly to come up with a plan to turn the sales around. Using demographics, I discovered that we were off on our target market. I immediately put together a proposal, and within a week we had a new marketing focus to reach the right customers. The new plan included coupons, two-for-ones, and special displays to attract customers. By the end of the month sales rose significantly.

    (B) I actually like change. In fact, I thrive on change. I am a person who can adapt easily to any situation you put me in. I was with one company where upper management changed three times in one year. I just don't let it get to me. I know how to roll with the punches. The worst thing for me is no change. To continue doing the same thing for years would really not be what I want from a job or career. Movement keeps me growing and learning; I like being challenged.

    (C) Change is something that happens every day in this industry. A policy difference can make everyone jump, and we have very little power over the situation. That has been one of the most frustrating things about my current job. There were just too many changes, without any thought behind them. I don't want to complain about management, but sometimes they changed the way we were doing something and then a week later changed it back to the way it had been before. That can be very frustrating for an employee.

ANSWERS
The Strongest Answer

(A) This is the strongest answer because it gives a very action-oriented example: There was a problem. You moved quickly to solve the problem. The problem was resolved. There is a strong sense of what your role was in the situation. This answer also would be a good reply to a question dealing with problem solving or coming up with a creative idea.

The Mediocre Answer

(B) This answer borders on being dangerous because it gives an impression of restlessness. Because you say that change is good but lack of change is deadly for you, the interviewer could get the impression that you aren't going to stick around long, particularly if this is a dead-end job.

The Weakest Answer

(C) This answer has a negative, whiny tone. It is a bad idea to bad-mouth former employers in an interview. Even if there were negative circumstances, it is best to let it go in the interview.

RATE YOURSELF

If you chose answer **(A)**, give yourself 5 points.

If you chose answer **(B)**, give yourself 3 points.

If you chose answer **(C)**, give yourself 0 points.   _____

It is not a good idea to speak negatively or "bad-mouth" a former boss or company in an interview. If you need to talk about a negative matter, speak only about the facts.

INTERVIEWER'S QUESTION

33. **"Can you give me an example of working in a fast-paced environment?"**

Select the strongest answer.

(A) I thrive on fast-paced environments where I am challenged to meet deadlines. The more pressure there is, the better I respond. I have been involved in as many as five projects at the same time, all with tight deadlines. I always learn from each project I accomplish and can apply the new information to the next project to be more efficient. I have the ability to think very quickly and respond to situations as needed, with a good sense of what is needed. I've never had an assignment in which I haven't succeeded. I have very good organizational skills and communications skills. I also have great computer skills that can help with the tracking of a project.

(B) When I was a support person in a law office, there was one time when we had to get everything ready for a case and were short-staffed because one of the other support persons was out ill. I took on the responsibility of coordinating all the reports. The first thing I did was sit down with the attorneys involved and ask them to give me an idea of the priorities that they needed to complete their part of the project. I then put together a task spreadsheet and worked with everyone to keep on track. We worked late into the night: 2:00 A.M. Instead of being tired, I felt energized throughout the experience. It was really rewarding when we finished the last task and made the deadline. Everyone was really surprised at how smoothly it went with all the obstacles I had to work around. I received a nice bonus for my efforts.

(C) We had this project to work on, and it seemed like everything was going wrong. First of all, we had a very tight deadline and were short a staff member. We had handled this type of pressure before, but this case was particularly important because it was one of our major clients. This case included a lot of visuals, such as charts and graphs and photos. The attorneys were really under a lot of pressure, and there was a lot of tension in the office. At one point I just felt like sitting down and crying, but I didn't. I just kept working through the anxiety and tension. I knew that if we didn't get this pulled together in time, there would be a very dissatisfied client. We all worked overtime that weekend, but we completed the job on time.

ANSWERS

The Strongest Answer

(B) This is the strongest answer because it provides a very good example of pitching in and getting something done. This example points out organizational skills, initiative, leadership, judgment, the ability to communicate, and a willingness to do "whatever it takes to get the job done." This story also provides an example of overcoming obstacles.

The Mediocre Answer

(A) This answer basically gives the same information that is given in answer (B), but without any examples. You say that you "have very good organizational and communications skills." Prove it. Give an example. Anybody can say that he or she is good at any task, but when you give a specific example of a time when you did the task, the interviewer gets a better idea of how you worked in the past.

The Weakest Answer

(C) This answer does not reveal any of your skills. There is too much emphasis on the problem without an explanation of your role. There are too many "we"s and not enough "I"s. The only direct reference to your behavior is when you talk about how stressed you were: "I just felt like sitting down and crying." The positive is that you said, "But I didn't," which indicates that you are not a quitter and that you have perseverance.

RATE YOURSELF

If you chose answer (B), give yourself 5 points.

If you chose answer (A), give yourself 3 points.

If you chose answer (C), give yourself 0 points.   _____

INTERVIEWER'S QUESTION

34. **"Have you been able to sell your boss on a new idea? How did you do it?"**

Select the strongest answer.

(A) My current boss is not very receptive to new ideas. I was able to sell her on one of my ideas when I showed her a marketing plan that I worked on to change some of the channels we were using for distribution. Behind the scenes I put together a lot of data and analysis that included details, facts, and figures. That extra effort really paid off when I presented her with the idea. She is one of those people who need facts to make decisions. She trusted me a lot more after that.

(B) My boss would tell you that I am always selling him on ideas. I have at least one idea a week. Some work, and some don't. My success rate is about 75 percent positive. One of the frustrations that I have is getting through the approval stage. When you work for a large company, it sometimes can take weeks to get an idea through the mill. I am an action-oriented guy who wants to make things happen. Sometimes it takes so long to get an idea through the channels that it is less effective than it would be if I had been able to start on it when I first had the idea.

(C) I determined a need to market a product by using a different strategy. I met with my boss to convince her of my ideas and she reluctantly gave me the go-ahead. I then met with the editorial, creative, and media departments. Working together, we planned media exposure, including TV, radio, print, newspaper, and interactive. We also put together a direct mail campaign. I calculated expenses and return on investment and presented it to my boss for approval. I really surprised her with the numbers and my estimated 30 percent return on investment. She gave a "thumbs-up" to proceed with the project.

ANSWERS

The Strongest Answer

(C) This is the strongest answer because of the strong example it gives of action on your part. The steps are laid out: the situation, the action you took, the results. Showing a positive outcome makes for a good success story. There are times, however, when the outcome may not be positive for the company for reasons that are completely out of your control. When this is the case, keep the focus on your role in the project and the way you completed your task. Do not dwell on the company's problems. This is about you and the skills you have to offer. Talk about what you were responsible for and how your part was finished successfully even if there were no positive results. An example would be a project that was shelved after you did all the work to complete it.

The Mediocre Answer

(A) This is not a bad answer, but it could be strengthened by more detail. Describing the analytic process and the types of facts and figures that you found and presented would be more effective. The good part of this story is your ability to understand that your boss has a style, which requires facts, and your ability to adapt your approach to meet her needs.

The Weakest Answer

(B) This answer is too general; it provides no facts. It also presents the complaining side of dealing with the process, which may or may not occur in the new job. It is best to ask questions about the process first and then judge whether this culture is going to be different from the one you just left.

RATE YOURSELF

If you chose answer **(C)**, give yourself 5 points.

If you chose answer **(A)**, give yourself 3 points.

If you chose answer **(B)**, give yourself 0 points.   _____

INTERVIEWER'S QUESTION

35. **"When was the last time you changed your personal style to adapt to someone ? Describe the situation."**
   Select the strongest answer.

   (A) Because I deal with a great many products and customers, I have to be very aware of the needs of the customer and act accordingly. For instance, I have some customers who are young and active and need clothes and shoes that correspond to their lifestyles. I make sure I know my customers and the needs of each individual. That has been a big part of my success in sales.

   (B) I worked with a group of young people who were looking for clothes to wear on a camping trip. Rather than give them a pitch about what they "should" have, I asked them a few questions and then listened to what they had to say. I heard things that I wouldn't have thought of if I had jumped right in with my pitch. Based on what I heard, I put together a selection to present to them at our next meeting. They were pleasantly surprised that I had heard their requests.

   (C) I consider this skill to be my major strength. I have the ability to change my personal style to adapt to the person I am working with. I take into consideration what the product is that I am trying to sell and who my customer is, and I adapt my style: the way I talk and what I say. This has been the most effective means for me to improve my communication skills and make more sales in the process.

ANSWERS
The Strongest Answer

(B) This answer provides the strongest example of a specific time when you adapted your style. It shows flexibility and the ability to know when to push and when to back off, which is an important trait in sales. It also demonstrates the ability to work with people of different ages and interests and do market research. Other skills shown are the ability to listen and the ability to follow through.

The Mediocre Answer

(A) This answer does not give a specific example, but it does give a "for instance" that, unfortunately, sounds generic. Although it talks about adaptability and customer service, it needs to show an actual example to be a stronger answer.

The Weakest Answer

(C) This is the weakest answer because it speaks in generalities. Like answer (A) it gives skills such as adaptability and judgment, but it provides no concrete evidence that you have done what you say you can do. This would be a much stronger answer if you related a story about a time when you adapted your style.

RATE YOURSELF

If you chose answer (B), give yourself 5 points.

If you chose answer (A), give yourself 3 points.

If you chose answer (C), give yourself 0 points.   _____

INTERVIEWER'S QUESTION

36. **"Give me an example of a time when you did more than the job required."**

Select the strongest answer.

(A) I am a person who likes to stay busy. When my workload is down, I try to organize to be more efficient. While processing claims one day, I had the idea that the salespeople could enter claims on-line and shorten the entire process. I put in some extra time designing a system that could be used as a prototype. I showed it to my boss, and she thought it was a great idea and design. In fact, she showed her boss. It eventually was incorporated into the company's process.

(B) Going above and beyond what is expected is something I do all the time. I always get excellent performance appraisals and do the job as required. I try to help people whenever they have a problem. I feel people are very important to our business, and I am very responsive to customer's problems. I am a very dedicated support person who can be depended on to do the job and give it my full attention.

(C) I am a person who plans ahead, and I always have a good handle on the workload. Because I am extremely organized, I am never late and meet all my deadlines. I pride myself on my dependability. I always plan ahead, using reminders to myself. I put in whatever time is required. My boss would tell you that I am very efficient and have a great attitude about getting my work done and doing whatever it takes.

ANSWERS
The Strongest Answer

(A) This is the strongest answer because it gives an example of a time when you went beyond what the job required. In this answer you show a very proactive approach to thinking of solutions to problems. This answer also could be used if you were asked about a time when you thought of a solution to a problem.

The Mediocre Answer

(B) This answer lacks a "specific" example. The ingredients for a good success story are there, but there is a need for detail. If you gave an example of a time when you went out of your way to help a customer with a problem, it would be a more relevant answer.

The Weakest Answer

(C) This is a weak answer because it is vague. It lists a lot of good skills but lacks examples of times when those skills were used. The strongest part of this answer is the quote from your boss. It always works well to have a "third party" endorse your work.

RATE YOURSELF

If you chose answer **(A)**, give yourself 5 points.

If you chose answer **(B)**, give yourself 3 points.

If you chose answer **(C)**, give yourself 0 points.   _____

By writing stories about your successes you will be prepared to answer a number of questions and show that you have performed similar work successfully in the past. Your stories about your experience are sometimes interchangeable and can be used to answer more than one question.

INTERVIEWER'S QUESTION

37. **"Give me an example of a time when you had to sacrifice quality to meet a deadline."**
Select the strongest answer.

(A) I can't think of a time when I ever missed a deadline. Deadlines are really important in our business. In fact, I would go so far as to say that my job was completely deadline-driven. I would have to plan my day to make sure that I did not miss deadlines. I recently was given an award for my record of keeping the customer satisfied by delivering the product on time.

(B) There was a tight deadline, but because of circumstances beyond our control we could not make the delivery date. I did a quick analysis and determined that the only way we could have met the deadline would have been to send the product without testing. I called the customer and explained the situation. I gave the customer a couple of alternatives with a recommendation to delay the shipping date to allow for proper testing. By giving the customer some time frames and cost figures, I was able to get them to agree to extend the deadline. In the end, the product was shipped within three days. The customer later thanked me for my judgment in the matter.

(C) Deadlines don't move; my workday does. When I have a deadline that looks tight, I have to work harder. I often have to work nights, sometimes as late as midnight, and sometimes on weekends. Quality may get sacrificed from time to time, but we always meet the deadlines. This is actually what I find most challenging about the job.

ANSWERS
The Strongest Answer

(B) This is the strongest answer. The deadline was not met, but the process for handling the problem makes this answer strong. The skills listed are meeting deadlines and include using judgment, problem solving, negotiating, initiative, and communication skills. One of the reasons this is the best answer is that it makes it clear what the problem was, what your role was, and how it turned out. This is a good example of a complete story.

The Mediocre Answer

(C) This answer isn't bad, but an interviewer might wonder why you need to work such long hours. Is it because you are short-staffed or constantly behind in your workload? This answer also indicates a focus on deadlines only, with little regard for quality. Each job and company will have a different need for quality versus quantity. Depending on the position and the job, make sure that you answer with the focus where it belongs.

The Weakest Answer

(A) This answer is weak because it indicates a focus on deadlines, not quality. In certain jobs where deadlines drive the business this answer may be appropriate. However, in this case the interviewer asked about quality and was not given a specific answer. Nevertheless, the mention of the award received is a positive point.

RATE YOURSELF

If you chose answer **(B)**, give yourself 5 points.

If you chose answer **(C)**, give yourself 3 points.

If you chose answer **(A)**, give yourself 0 points.   _____

INTERVIEWER'S QUESTION

38. **"What has been the most difficult training course or class you've ever taken?"**
Select the strongest answer.

   (A) I don't know if you want to consider the classes I took while I was getting my BA degree, but I had a couple of classes that were killers. I was carrying a full load of credits and working a 30-hour week. I had a geology class that was the most difficult class I ever took. The way I survived was to plan the projects and study times, and I would stick to the plan no matter what. Because that class was the most difficult, I made sure that it was my main focus that semester. Focus was the key to surviving that course.

   (B) I can't think of one course that was more difficult than the others. I have taken a lot of training courses since I graduated from college. Because I pick up things easily and quickly, I move right along. The classes and courses I have enjoyed the most have been about finance and investing. I have a good mind for numbers and theory, and that has helped me in my previous positions. I intend to keep taking classes as a way of to develop new techniques.

   (C) I've taken a lot of training courses in my career. Some of them have had to do with business, some with personal growth, and some with technology. I enjoy a broad coverage of subjects. I'm a strong believer in continuous training. I guess the most difficult programs have been in the area of technology, which probably is my weakest area.

ANSWERS
The Strongest Answer

(A) This is the strongest answer because it is the most specific. Even though it is not about business, it gives a good example of how you focused your efforts to get through a tough situation. It is desirable to give a business answer as your first choice, but if you can't think of a situation that answers the question, give an answer that is as closely related to the question as possible. This is especially true for new grads or reentry persons. This answer indicates your ability to be organized and plan as well as defining your tenacity. The skills demonstrated are the important aspect of this example.

The Mediocre Answer

(C) This answer is not wrong; it is just not a strong answer. On the positive side it does include the various kinds of training you've taken. In answer to this particular question it would sound better if you focused on a specific course that challenged you the most. You say that the technology classes were the most difficult but don't give any of the specifics that would add depth to your answer.

The Weakest Answer

(B) This is the weakest answer because it does not answer the question. It is very general. It has some merit because it speaks about your ability to learn quickly and pick up information easily. It also demonstrates an ethic of continuous growth through learning, which is positive.

RATE YOURSELF

If you chose answer (A), give yourself 5 points.

If you chose answer (C), give yourself 3 points.

If you chose answer (B), give yourself 0 points.   _____

INTERVIEWER'S QUESTION

39. **"Give me an example of a marketing strategy you've used."**
    Select the strongest answer.

   (A) My company made a special offer to customers, and it wasn't going well. I was the new account manager and was given the program, which had been running in the red for over a year. We did a lot of analysis, and we found out some information about the customer base and discovered that we were targeting the wrong offer to the wrong consumer. When this happens, we have to work hard to get the customer to try our product again. This time we offered a better program with more cost savings. Because of the economy we realized that people were being thrifty with their purchases, and we hadn't taken that factor into consideration when the product was launched. We were able to turn the situation around in the end.

   (B) When I was the account manager in my last position, I was given a program that had been operating in the red for over a year. The problem was that my company had come up with an offer to the customer, offering a higher quality of merchandise and more points for buying. As it turned out, we were targeting the wrong customer base. When the customers clicked on the website and saw such pricey merchandise, they were dropping out of the program rather than buying more. It was a very challenging situation for me, but I was able to turn it around quickly.

   (C) I came into a situation as the account manager on a program that has been operating in the red for over a year. I had to identify the issues and problem quickly. I began by looking at the profit and loss statements. Once I got the numbers, I discovered that a program that offered a higher-quality product to consumers was not being accepted, partly because of the economy. I was able to quickly put in place a new program that offered customers cost savings instead. By focusing more on what the customer needed and the financial picture, I was able to turn the situation around in a short time.

ANSWERS
The Strongest Answer

(C) This is the strongest answer because it is very specific and detailed. The problem is well defined, and the presentation is balanced. The answer demonstrates analysis and quick action to change a situation. You were successful in solving a problem and have given a good example of how you work in a negative situation.

The Mediocre Answer

(B) This is not the strongest answer because the emphasis is on the problem, with very little action or information about what you did. What was your role? What action did you take? This story is too heavy on the situation and too light on the action, with only a brief mention of the result. Stories should be balanced, with the action having the most detail.

The Weakest Answer

(A) This answer is the weakest because it is a "we" story rather than an "I" story. Read it again and you will find that there are seven "we"s and one "I." It is difficult for the interviewer to get a sense of your work if you don't talk about your role and what you did.

RATE YOURSELF

If you chose answer (C), give yourself 5 points.

If you chose answer (B), give yourself 3 points.

If you chose answer (A), give yourself 0 points.   _____

INTERVIEWER'S QUESTION

40. **"Tell me about a time when you helped in the development of a coworker or subordinate."**
    Select the strongest answer.

    (A) I had a dotted-line responsibility for the support staff in my department. One of the women was really struggling with her workload. I talked to her and found out she was having problems at home; because she hadn't been able to attend some training classes, she was trying to pick up the information on her own. She agreed to work with me during her lunch hour or any time she could spare. I laid out a plan for her to follow and coached her on sections that needed explanation. She was a quick learner and came up to speed in less than three weeks. She was very grateful for my extra attention, and I was pleased with her performance improvement.

    (B) My coaching skills are one of my strengths. I have coached several people inside and outside my department. Employees know that they can come to me for answers, and as a result they seek me out. One of my basic rules when helping people is that they have to have tried to work their problems out on their own first. I can tell when someone is frustrated beyond the point of self-help and will try to work with him or her at that point. I don't believe in holding someone's hand, but I will help if an honest attempt has been made.

    (C) I recently helped a coworker who was having real problems with the new system for tracking calls. She had missed some of the training sessions and was running behind with the new procedures. We were all so used to the old system that we could do it in a robotic state. But this new system was really complicated. The company put us through four weeks of training to learn the system, and even though I attended all the sessions, I had to put in extra effort to learn the details. She and I worked together, and she improved very quickly.

ANSWERS
The Strongest Answer

(A) This is the strongest answer because it provides a clear example of not only developing someone but going the extra mile to do so. This story is clear, with an explanation of the situation, a plan for carrying out the action, and a result or the outcome. This is also an example of a story that would work if you were asked, "Tell me about a time when you went above and beyond what the job called for."

The Mediocre Answer

(C) This is not as strong an answer as (A) because it spends too much time explaining the problem and does not provide enough detail on the action or solution. There is very little evidence of what you did to help your coworker. This is a very common problem in relating behavioral stories. Spending more time on the action of the story (at least 60 percent) than on the problem or the result is crucial.

The Weakest Answer

(B) This answer is not focused on developing or helping anyone in particular. It gives a lot of detail about your philosophy of teaching or coaching but provides little evidence that you actually have helped an individual. The interviewer does not have a clear picture of a time when you helped develop someone's skills.

RATE YOURSELF

If you chose answer (A), give yourself 5 points.

If you chose answer (C), give yourself 3 points.

If you chose answer (B), give yourself 0 points. _____

INTERVIEWER'S QUESTION

41. **"Tell me about a time when you coordinated a project or event."**
    Select the strongest answer.

    (A) I led a project to roll out a new product. A new exclusive pack was being marketed for a specific store. One of the important factors was working closely with the finance department on a financial analysis. The challenge was to accomplish our goal within budget and still meet the customer's needs. We did primary and secondary research in order to do a competitive analysis of similar products. We were able to present the conclusions and recommendations successfully to top-level management with positive results.

    (B) I led the rollout of a new product for an exclusive pack to be featured in a major retail store. The first thing I did was to open channels of communication by meeting with the members of my team, letting them know as much detail about the project as I could. Next, I collaborated closely with all the other departments involved in the project. Through team efforts I was able to get primary and secondary research for the new product against the competition. We presented our results and recommendations to upper-level management for final approval and got strong commendations for our work as a team.

    (C) I have been the lead on several new product rollouts. I always make sure that my team is informed. I also make sure that I am working collaboratively with the other departments, such as finance and the departments responsible for the supply chain. When I work on these types of projects, it is very important to me that we are on schedule and that all deadlines are met. My team is very responsive to my direction because the members know I deliver results. My main rule when coordinating a project is to keep the lines of communication open.

ANSWERS
The Strongest Answer

(B) This is the strongest answer because of the specifics given in answering the question. This answer goes through the steps to complete the process and show how you work with others. Strong leadership and coordination skills are demonstrated clearly. Note that even though this was a team effort, you were able to demonstrate your role and use the word "I."

The Mediocre Answer

(A) This is not as strong an answer because it focuses primarily on the problem and gives very little detail about the steps taken. When you focus too heavily on the project or situation, you tend to stray from the subject and end up missing the opportunity to sell yourself.

The Weakest Answer

(C) This is the weakest answer because it only roughly explains how you coordinated a project. All the right skills are present, but you don't bring up specific examples of how you achieved results. The fatal flaw in this answer is that it does not mention the results or the outcome at all.

RATE YOURSELF

If you chose answer **(B),** give yourself 5 points.

If you chose answer **(A),** give yourself 3 points.

If you chose answer **(C),** give yourself 0 points.   _____

INTERVIEWER'S QUESTION

42. **"Describe a time when you had to make an unpopular decision."**
Select the strongest answer.

(A) In my analyst job I worked with a team whose task it was to target productivity studies. We had to explore all avenues and options in solving problems and making recommendations. This sometimes included laying people off. We labored over our decisions so that we would be fair and objective. We then had to present our findings to upper management and stand by our decisions even though they sometimes were challenged. Most of our recommendations were accepted and resulted in a decreased labor cost of 30 percent.

(B) I thoroughly explore all avenues in targeting productivity studies. Only as a last resort would I recommend laying people off, which probably is considered the most unpopular decision a manager can make. Sometimes I make recommendations for procedural changes that can be unpopular with employees. Change often is viewed negatively. The more popular recommendations that I have made include streamlining procedures and saving money and time by computerizing processes.

(C) Decisions affecting people's lives are the most difficult. As part of my last job I conducted a productivity study that determined that some jobs were redundant. I was in charge of a committee that would decide who would be laid off. As the team's leader I was responsible for putting together the basic criteria for the decision. I did an analysis of the positions and people, their seniority, their salaries, and their job content. The group had to make decisions on the basis of the standards I set up. It went smoothly and resulted in a 30 percent cost saving, but it didn't make the decisions any easier.

ANSWERS

The Strongest Answer

(C) This is the strongest answer because it gives a detailed picture of your actions in putting together the criteria to make a strong decision; this shows the interviewer that you are willing to take on a task even though it may not be popular with the rest of the employees. This is a good example of your leadership and preparedness. It is also a strong answer because it is quantified. Whenever possible, quantify, or give a number, to establish the scope of the situation.

The Mediocre Answer

(A) This answer is not as strong because there is no indication of your role in this example. Even when you were part of a team, you need to convey what you did as a team member. When you talk about the situation, be sure to include yourself and your role in the project as part of the story.

The Weakest Answer

(B) This answer is the weakest because it lacks focus. It starts out well, takes a turn down a different road, and ends up on the positive and popular side of examples when the question clearly asked for a specific time when you made an "unpopular" decision. Thinking about the question and focusing on one or two points will make the answer more succinct.

RATE YOURSELF

If you chose answer **(C)**, give yourself 5 points.

If you chose answer **(A)**, give yourself 3 points.

If you chose answer **(B)**, give yourself 0 points.   _____

Most interviewers will remember only one or two points from your story. Make sure that your story is focused and that it answers the question asked. When you stray from the original example, you confuse the interviewer.

INTERVIEWER'S QUESTION

43. **"Tell me about the most creative project you've worked on."**
    Select the strongest answer.

 (A) I created a multimedia lecture series that was based on the history of film by incorporating film footage from various movies and TV shows through the years to support me with some of the new things that I was attempting. I came up with an idea for presenting the award-winning films through the last 50 years of film and showing how computerization could have changed the effect. Then I used the techniques used today to demonstrate how far film has advanced. The crew I worked with gave me great praise for my original way of presenting the idea, using the latest technology available.

 (B) I try to put a new spin on all my projects instead of repeating the same old stuff. I did a project recently on the history of film that turned out better than expected. My secret to being creative is to look at what's been done before and then try something completely new. I am known for my originality and creativity among my peers and others I have worked with. I have worked nationally and internationally and have a broad view of what it takes to be creative in this business.

 (C) In my business it is especially important to "think out of the box." Every project I work on presents a new challenge. Whether I'm working with private collections or museum displays or working on live-action short films, I am excited by the challenge of the medium. I am known for my work with film and have been praised by all concerned, including my camera crews.

ANSWERS

The Strongest Answer

(A) This answer provides a clear example of what you did and the methods you used to accomplish a successful outcome. This is also a good example of letting the interviewer know that you have done this type of work before and can do it again. Mentioning that the crew thought highly of your work is a good way to provide an endorsement from people who worked with you.

The Mediocre Answer

(B) This answer isn't as strong as (A) because it is not as crisp and clear. It touches on a specific project but doesn't provide the details that will let the interviewer know the skills used and your method of working. This answer has some good material but needs more detail to show a good picture of you.

The Weakest Answer

(C) This answer fails to focus on creativity. It shows a definite interest in film and enthusiasm for different media but does not mention any projects you worked on that would tell the interviewer specifically how you carried out your creative work. Even the endorsement given is too general to be of much significance.

RATE YOURSELF

If you chose answer **(A)**, give yourself 5 points.

If you chose answer **(B)**, give yourself 3 points.

If you chose answer **(C)**, give yourself 0 points.   _____

INTERVIEWER'S QUESTION

44. **"You say you have good customer service skills. Tell me about a time when you used good customer service skills in your job."**
Select the strongest answer.

(A) Good customer service is the name of the game, and I believe that the internal customers and the external customers are equally important. The first rule of good customer service is that you have to take care of your customer or your account will take its business elsewhere. I try to make the customer right every time, within reason. We have to live by our corporate rules, and even if they are unreasonable, we do our best to hold to company policy. I try to work as a liaison between corporate and the sales reps, smoothing out problems.

(B) I resolved a customer problem that involved one of our sales reps and another company. I worked as a liaison between our rep and the corporate office. The rep was very upset because we weren't standing behind our warranty on a product he sold to that company. The first thing I did was to pull the appropriate paperwork, and then I made a recommendation to our corporate office. I laid out the facts, and we had a bit of a negotiation. In the end everything turned out well for the rep and the customer. The rep couldn't thank me enough. He said that I saved the account.

(C) In my 10 years working with customers I have had numerous compliments on my service skills from my customers and reps. I often work directly with customers, and sometimes I work as a liaison between our sales reps and corporate. Because I am a person who is very organized and pays attention to details, I am able to pull together the facts and present the case in a more organized manner. This process not only empowers me to do what I can do to help, it also gives my reps a feeling that someone is on their side.

ANSWERS

The Strongest Answer

(B) This is the strongest answer because it answers the question with a good example of your work as a liaison between the sales reps (your customer) and corporate and the way you used a number of good customer service skills. Some of the skills demonstrated are research, organization, and negotiation skills. It also provides a good example of taking the initiative and recommending a solution rather than asking for advice and putting the problem on corporate.

The Mediocre Answer

(C) This is not a bad answer; it just is not specific enough. The answer speaks about skills but does not give an example. The interviewer asks for proof or backup of the claim that you have good customer service skills. Any time you mention a skill on your résumé or during an interview, the interviewer may ask you to prove it with an example

The Weakest Answer

(A) This answer is the weakest one because it preaches to the interviewer. The interviewer already knows that customer service is important and that if people are not good with customer service, the company will lose business. Another negative aspect of this answer is that it complains about corporate policy and the need to follow it in spite of its being unreasonable. This is not a good tone to take in an interview because it could indicate that you are someone who is passive and does the work but really does not believe in what the company stands for. There are many companies to choose from; it is best to determine which company's business philosophy is in line with yours as much as possible. An example of a bad match is an environmentally concerned person going to work for a pesticide company.

RATE YOURSELF

If you chose answer **(B)**, give yourself 5 points.

If you chose answer **(C)**, give yourself 3 points.

If you chose answer **(A)**, give yourself 0 points.   _____

INTERVIEWER'S QUESTION

45. **"Tell me about a time when your communication skills made a difference."**
Select the strongest answer.

(A) My skills are strong in written and oral communications. I write a great deal of the curriculum for teaching programs. I've worked with great teams and focused on the invaluable role of art as a source of cultural enrichment in our everyday lives. I have written interactive exercises and developed creative test models that are used as standards in the schools where I have worked. Communication with the teams I have worked with has made a huge difference in the success of my projects. I couldn't have done it without their cooperation and communication.

(B) I have over five years of experience developing and delivering programs for schools. I develop, organize, and conduct educational tour programs to Europe, focusing on relaying the role of art and history as cultural enrichments in our everyday lives. I cowrote and helped produce a series of art videos that are used in educational institutions throughout the United States. I am known for my passionate delivery and presentation of materials that have been viewed as uninteresting when presented by others. It's the way you present the information that makes the difference.

(C) One project I worked on involved developing the curriculum for a program dealing with cultural similarities in everyday life. The challenge was to communicate with my team members and get them as excited about their roles in the project as I was about mine. I talked to them individually, drawing out the particular interests they had. I used this information to assign responsibilities where there was interest, enabling me to bring about extremely positive results through a team effort. The feedback from the team was that every person felt he or she had made a contribution in his or her own special way. It was worth the extra effort taken to listen and obtain their input.

ANSWERS

The Strongest Answer

(C) This is the strongest answer because of the focus on the way you used communication skills to work with individuals, listening and implementing the ideas heard. Because good communication skills involve listening and writing as well as speaking, you have demonstrated a broad use of your skills. This is an answer that also shows strong leadership skills as well as the ability to appreciate the differences people bring to a situation.

The Mediocre Answer

(A) This answer has all the makings of a good story; it just needs to be rearranged to focus on the communication issues and address the question. If you compare this example with the stronger answer (C), you can see how the same information is given, but with more emphasis placed on communication with the team that brought about successful results.

The Weakest Answer

(B) This answer speaks about your experiences as they are written on your résumé, not as a relevant example of your experience. A specific example of any one of the skills you mentioned would be stronger than reiterating your résumé content. The last part of this answer could be developed as an example of your presentation to a group and the feedback you obtained about your passionate delivery.

RATE YOURSELF

If you chose answer (C), give yourself 5 points.

If you chose answer (A), give yourself 3 points.

If you chose answer (B), give yourself 0 points.   _____

The Interview IQ Test

INTERVIEWER'S QUESTION

46. "Describe the assignment that required you to take care of the greatest number of details."
Select the strongest answer.

(A) You can't do the type of work I do and not pay strong attention to details. I am known for being very accurate. In fact, my team members bring me their work to check for accuracy. I have a natural eye for detail. I have always been great at proofreading and picking up errors. I have worked on statements with thousands of figures, and I have just kept at it until I have all the entries correct. One time it took me a week of tedious checking of facts and numbers, but in the end I had a quality product. It would bother me a lot if my work went out with errors.

(B) I recently worked on a project that included lots of details. The way I work is to set up spreadsheets and track the details and my progress. By making sure that all the entries are correct and that I meet my deadline, I have had great success with projects. My last project made a big difference in the efficiency of customer repair orders. I pride myself on checking and rechecking details whenever I am working on a project. Sometimes I have my teammates check my work to make sure that I haven't made any mistakes. On my performance appraisals my boss always mentions what great attention to detail I use.

(C) I set up an in-house tracking system for customer repair units. I organized all the data collected to date and entered the times the order was taken against the time elapsed before the repair was complete. It was important to assure accuracy in the initial setup of this system, and so I hand sorted and entered all the information myself and had a team member check my entries. We ran a trial run to assure that everything was working, and the results were flawless. This project reduced the turnaround time on customer orders by 50 percent. I was given a lot of praise for my precise work, and I also received a nice bonus.

ANSWERS
The Strongest Answer

(C) This is the strongest answer because of the detail given. There is a strong indication of a need to be accurate but not compulsive. The answer also shows other qualities, such as being organized and collaborating with other team members. By quantifying the savings made to the company and the rewards given, you make a stronger impact.

The Mediocre Answer

(B) This answer is not as strong because it places the emphasis of the story in the wrong place and buries the most important information. It starts out by being specific and then lapses into general information. By saying, "My last project made a big difference in the efficiency of customer repair orders," you have minimized the effect of the project. Answer (C) states that the project reduced the turnaround time by 50 percent, which is far more specific and impressive.

The Weakest Answer

(A) This is the weakest answer because it lacks specific details but also may be seen as somewhat compulsive. By giving a specific example of a time when you had a project with detail, you would soften the impact of "always having to be accurate."

RATE YOURSELF

If you chose answer (C), give yourself 5 points.

If you chose answer (B), give yourself 3 points.

If you chose answer (A), give yourself 0 points.   _____

INTERVIEWER'S QUESTION

47. **"Give me an example of taking care of business day to day but also thinking long-range."**
Select the strongest answer.

(A) I am a project manager who keeps an eye on what's going on in the general market. Sometimes I have to respond quickly to get the market share, particularly in a tight economy. I usually spend a great deal of time working on the budget, attempting to maximize leverage. I've been known to take risks such as purchasing expensive advertising to get the word out. I am willing to do whatever it takes to compete in the market and feel that in the long run this will pay off. I've had experience leading some very successful campaigns even when market conditions weren't in our favor.

(B) Customer retention was a big challenge in my last company. I worked with my staff and members of other relevant departments to strategize ways to retain first and build second. Teams were sent out to interview customers, and the data collected were given to the marketing department for analysis. We obtained feedback from our customers stating that they wanted to be asked first or wanted information on request only. They didn't like our current telemarketing campaign and were annoyed because they were receiving information they didn't want or need. By working collaboratively and involving other departments, I was able to see a day-to-day problem with an impact on the bigger picture.

(C) I've had a lot of experience with long-range planning, particularly in the area of product branding. We hired some star athletes to "brand" our product. We sold the brand name, and everything we did pushed the name. We bought mailing lists and sent out thousands of ads through the mail and e-mail. We spent a fair share of our budget pushing the brand. Every activity we did during the campaign revolved around this brand. We were trying to establish a presence, and we did. We focused on the present and the day-to-day activities on this project, and it paid off.

ANSWERS

The Strongest Answer

(B) This is the strongest answer. It is succinct and to the point. It talks about a specific problem and mentions the solution. The example indicates your ability to see the day-to-day issues while keeping an eye on the future and doing that by working with teams and departments across functions to get the maximum impact.

The Mediocre Answer

(A) This is not as strong an answer because it does not focus on or address the question directly. The answer could be strengthened by adding an example of one of those "successful campaigns" you talk about.

The Weakest Answer

(C) This is a weak answer because of its overuse of the pronoun "we." If you count, you can find nine "we"s, which is too many to include if you want to show what your role was in this process. Even though you were working with teams and other departments, it is important that the interviewer hear your action in the activities.

RATE YOURSELF

If you chose answer **(B)**, give yourself 5 points.

If you chose answer **(A)**, give yourself 3 points.

If you chose answer **(C)**, give yourself 0 points.   _____

INTERVIEWER'S QUESTION

48. **"Give me a specific example of a time when you took the initiative."**
Select the strongest answer.

(A) When I took over the department in my last job, there were turnover problems. I sat down with the staff members and asked them why so many people were leaving. I learned that when they were hired, they were told that there would be cross-functional training and it never happened. I consider my team to be my main customer, and I immediately set a plan in motion. It involved presenting my plan to top management and requesting extra time and money. I put my job on the line, but I got what we needed. I turned the department around and bought some strong loyalty from my staff.

(B) I attempted to initiate things in my last company, but nobody was really interested in what I had to say. I always volunteer and am glad to help in any way that I can, but I don't want to take the responsibility for initiating projects. The last time I initiated something for a company, I got stuck with all the responsibility and work. I gave up trying to do something other than my job. Don't get me wrong. I am a hard worker and am more than willing to pull my weight, but I let other people lead.

(C) This is an example from my life outside of my job, but it is a project that I am very proud of. I was responsible for initiating a clothing drive for the homeless in our city. It came about when we were talking at lunch one day. There is a woman who hangs out near our building, and we all felt sorry for her because it was getting cold. Some of us had clothes and blankets that we were glad to donate, but we didn't know exactly how to approach the situation. I volunteered to research the situation and set up a drive. Some of my coworkers volunteered to help. By the end of the month we had collected so many coats and blankets that we presented them to the city for the shelters. We got a commendation from the mayor.

ANSWERS

The Strongest Answer

(A) This is the strongest answer because it gives a good example of stepping up to the plate and initiating action—getting things done. This is a strong example of being a good leader who takes the time to listen and respond. It is also an answer that shows strong qualities for motivating others and handling groups.

The Mediocre Answer

(C) This is not a bad answer. If you don't have a work-related experience to talk about, talking about a volunteer or personal situation is reasonable as long as it is appropriate in regard to the question asked. In this case you took the initiative to set up and research a program to help others.

The Weakest Answer

(B) This is the weakest answer because of the tone more than the content. It sounds negative and angry. It's not so much what is said but the impression it gives. If you don't want to lead, that is acceptable, but try to focus on the positive side of what you've done in the interview. Negative attitudes are a real turnoff for interviewers.

RATE YOURSELF

If you chose answer **(A)**, give yourself 5 points.

If you chose answer **(C)**, give yourself 3 points.

If you chose answer **(B)**, give yourself 0 points.   _____

INTERVIEWER'S QUESTION

49. **"Tell me about a time when you were driven to achieve and succeed."**
    Select the strongest answer.

    (A) I am driven by my own success. When I am performing well, I am driven to do better. We write marketing plans and goals each quarter, and I live by those plans, attempting to make as many calls and sales as I have projected. If I fall behind in my calls, I have to readjust my plan to make up for the slack, and this drives me even harder. It works well for me. I feel good about succeeding and am driven to continue as long as I continue to get results and am rewarded for my efforts.

    (B) Competition is usually a great driver for me. The more incentive is offered to me by the company, the more I am driven toward results. I can motivate myself by setting quotas to make a certain amount of calls every day, but it helps if there is a reward in the line of a bonus or percentage of sales to drive me harder. I work hard and do whatever it takes to maintain my accounts. I believe the secret to good sales is persistence and follow-up. I have built a reputation for being there for my customers.

    (C) I needed to stimulate interest with my customers and decided to hold a competition. I personally had accumulated a ton of frequent-flier miles and came up with the idea of offering an incentive for customers to let me introduce the new product. The deal was that every customer who let me demonstrate the product was entered into a drawing for a trip to Hawaii. I sent out letters and e-mails explaining the contest and had great results. I knew that once I was able to demonstrate the product, I could sell it. I came in tops in my division.

ANSWERS

The Strongest Answer

(C) This is the strongest answer because it shows original thinking and presents a strong example of a time when you were driven to succeed. This answer can be used to answer other questions, such as "Tell me about a time when you came up with a creative strategy" or "Tell me about a time when you thought out of the box."

The Mediocre Answer

(A) This answers talks about being driven and motivated but does not give a specific example to make it stronger. Self-motivation is a good quality to use in your stories, but anyone can say he or she is self-motivated. When you give an example of an actual time when you were driven as you did in answer (C), it has a stronger impact.

The Weakest Answer

(B) This is a weak answer that dwells on what kind of incentive the company can give you to motivate and drive you rather than the way you drive yourself. The interview should focus on what you can do for the company, not what the company can do for you.

RATE YOURSELF

If you chose answer (C), give yourself 5 points.

If you chose answer (A), give yourself 3 points.

If you chose answer (B), give yourself 0 points.   _____

INTERVIEWER'S QUESTION

50. **"Tell me about the most difficult sale you had to make. What did you do to get the sale?"**
Select the strongest answer.

(A) The first thing I do in a difficult sales situation is talk to the decision maker. I recently talked with a man who had started the business himself and took pride in his product. I acknowledged his accomplishment and inquired what the next level of sales for his business would be. He told me he was expanding and adding a delivery service. Before I could tell him what I had to offer, I asked a lot more questions about his vision and listened carefully to what he said. I had to get his trust before he would share his plans. Taking time to ask questions and listen carefully has made a huge difference in my success. I was able to sell him a bigger ad than he originally planned to buy.

(B) This is the challenge of sales: selling to customers when they are not necessarily receptive to buying. I have been in this business almost 10 years, and the majority of my sales have been difficult. When you call a business, you can get the same old response of "not interested." What I do is develop a plan for myself to hit a certain amount of calls per day. By setting a goal for myself I focus on the goal, not on the rejection. I've been at it long enough to know the techniques that can overcome objections and get me an appointment. Once I get the appointment, I know how to sell.

(C) The first thing I do when I am trying to sell a product, whether to an individual or to a company, is to find out their needs and what they will do with the product. I do this by listening to the needs of the customer and sometimes reading between the lines. I always reiterate what I heard through active listening. The customer responds well to my being able to "hear" his or her problem. Once I have established the need, I can begin to talk about my product as the solution to the problem. I have established great rapport with customers by using this technique.

ANSWERS
The Strongest Answer

(A) This is the strongest answer because it not only talks about your sales technique but provides a clear example of a successful sale. The example given shows a lot of patience and customer savvy on your part, recognizing that timing and trust are everything when you are selling someone a new product or idea.

The Mediocre Answer

(C) Although this answer has good content, it does not provide a specific example. This answer would get the point across if it included an application of the theory it outlines. Do you recognize the theory as being the way you should approach the job interview? Listen to "their" problem before you sell yourself as the solution to the problem. This is a basic sales technique.

The Weakest Answer

(B) This is the weakest answer because it describes your basic selling philosophy rather than your method of operation. Instead of talking about a specific difficult sale, you are focusing on your techniques and how you go about preparing for a sale. You are saying that you can overcome objections but are not giving any concrete examples of your successes.

RATE YOURSELF

If you chose answer **(A)**, give yourself 5 points.

If you chose answer **(C)**, give yourself 3 points.

If you chose answer **(B)**, give yourself 0 points.   _____

Demonstrating confidence and enthusiasm during the interview will have a big impact on your performance and the impression you leave behind.

What's Your Interview IQ?: Scorecard

Insert your score for each question in the blank following it. Then calculate your total points for all 50 questions.

GENERAL QUESTIONS

1. "Let's begin with you telling me about yourself." _____

2. "Why did you leave (*or* why are you planning to leave) your last position?" _____

3. "Why do you want to work here?" _____

4. "What are your goals?" _____

5. "What are your strengths?" _____

6. "What is your greatest weakness?" _____

7. "When have you been most motivated?" _____

8. "How would you describe your personality?" _____

9. "Have you ever been fired?" _____

10. "Why has it taken you so long to find a job" _____

11. "What experience do you have that qualifies you for this position?" _____

12. "How would your current or last boss describe your job performance?" _____

13. "What do you know about this company?" _____

14. "What do you think are the key qualities for a support person?" _____

15. "Describe your leadership or management style." _____

16. "In what ways has your current or last job prepared you to take on more responsibility?" _____

17. "What do you value most in a teammate?" _____

18. "What are the most important things for you in any job or company?" _____

19. "How do you stay current and informed about industry trends and technology?" _____

20. "Do you believe you're overqualified for this position?" _____

21. "If I asked your coworkers to say three positive things about you, what would they say?" _____

22. "Why should we hire you?" _____

23. "If I remember only one thing about you, what should that be?" _____

24. "What are your salary expectations?" _____

25. "Do you have any questions?" _____

BEHAVIORAL QUESTIONS

26. "Tell me about the biggest project you've worked on from start to finish." _____

27. "Tell me about a time when you had to overcome obstacles to get your job done." _____

28. "Tell me about a time when you had to handle a stressful situation." _____

29. "Your résumé states that you're a 'hard worker.' Can you give me an example of a time when you worked hard?" _____

30. "Tell me about a time when you had a disagreement/ confrontation with a boss or coworker." _____

31. "What was the most difficult problem you've handled? How did you deal with it?" _____

32. "Tell me about a time when you had to adapt quickly to a change." _____

33. "Can you give me an example of working in a fast-paced environment?" _____

34. "Have you been able to sell your boss on a new idea? How did you do it?" _____

35. "When was the last time you changed your personal style to adapt to someone? Describe the situation." _____

36. "Give me an example of a time when you did more than the job required." _____

37. "Give me an example of a time when you had to sacrifice quality to meet a deadline." _____

38. "What has been the most difficult training course or class you've ever taken?" _____

39. "Give me an example of a marketing strategy you've used." _____

40. "Tell me about a time when you helped in the development of a coworker or subordinate." _____

41. "Tell me about a time when you coordinated a project or event." _____

42. "Describe a time when you had to make an unpopular decision." _____

43. "Tell me about the most creative project you've worked on." _____

44. "You say you have good customer service skills. Tell me about a time when you used good customer service skills in your job." _____

45. "Tell me about a time when your communication skills made a difference." _____

46. "Describe the assignment that required you to take care of the greatest number of details." _____

47. "Give me an example of taking care of business day to day but also thinking long-range." _____

48. "Give me a specific example of a time when you took the initiative." _____

49. "Tell me about a time when you were driven to achieve and succeed." _____

50. "Tell me about the most difficult sale you had to make. What did you do to get the sale?" _____

Total Points _____

Rate Yourself: Point Evaluation

Evaluate your total points as follows.

Interview Ability Rating Point System

- **176 to 250 points: Genius Level**
You've got the idea. Now use your technique to prepare your own stories.

- **100 to 175 points: Above-Average Level**
The "story" format will enhance your answers and give you more success in the interview. Read Part 2 and then retake the test. You will be ready to prepare your own stories.

- **Below 100 points: Average Level**
It's okay to start out at this level. Preparation and practice will only improve your stories, your confidence, and your results. Read Part 2 and retake the test until you have achieved a higher score. Then write your own stories.

PART 2

The Surefire Way to Boost Your Score

Step 1:
Understanding Today's Interviewing Techniques

Unlocking the Secrets to Successful Interviewing

Above all, the secret to success in any interview is preparation. Can you imagine making a presentation to a group of people without knowing what you were going to say? Probably not. But how do you prepare for an interview when you don't know what the topic will be? How can you know what they will ask you? The answers to these questions will be revealed in the following sections.

Although there is no way to predict what you will be asked in an interview, there are preparation steps that will help you deal with the questions that will be asked. This is especially true if behavioral interviewing techniques are used.

What Is Behavioral Interviewing?

Let's start with a discussion of what behavioral interviewing is and why it is important to be able to determine whether you are being asked behavioral questions. Behavioral interviewing is an interviewing technique employers use to determine whether a candidate is a good fit for

the job. The technique involves questions that determine your behavior—
in particular, your past behavior—as an indicator of your future success.
In other words, the answers you give about your past experiences will be
used to predict your future performance: If you did it before, you can do
it again. This includes both positive and negative behavior.

A Brief History of Behavioral Interviewing

Before we discuss creating your own stories, let's start by examining the
reason companies use behavioral interviewing techniques. In the 1970s
industrial psychologists developed a new way to predict accurately
whether a person would succeed in a job. On the basis of the principle
that future performance can be predicted by examining past behavior,
candidates were asked questions that requested proof, often in the form
of examples, that they had done what they claimed to be able to do.

Research performed over the last three decades indicates that when
only traditional interview questions are asked during an interview, up to
75 percent of the people hired do not meet the performance expectations
after they start the job. Some candidates interview well, but when it comes
to performance, they aren't who they claimed to be. According to an arti-
cle titled "Improve at the Interview" in the February 3, 2003, issue of
Business Week, companies that have adopted behavioral interviewing
techniques claim to make better hiring decisions and to have as much as
five times more success with retention and performance than they were
getting when they used the traditional interviewing style.

In today's job market, in which employers have so many applicants to
choose from, they must make accurate hiring decisions and rely on more
effective ways to screen candidates. Because of costly hiring mistakes,
employers have become more cautious about hiring on the basis of "gut
feelings." According to *Business Week*, standard interviews have a 7 percent rate of accuracy in their predictions as opposed to situational interviewing, which includes role playing and behavioral interviewing
techniques, which increases accuracy in predicting performance by as
much as 54 percent.

An interviewer uses behavioral interviewing techniques to draw out
specific examples of a job candidate's past behavior to determine the candidate's ability to perform in similar circumstances. In other words, what
past behavior can this person bring to this company? What successes will
be repeated in this job? Will the skills and knowledge this person already
possesses save the company time, money, or labor power?

As the interviewer finds out more about the way you act, your
method of operation, and how you handle situations, a profile or picture

of you is formed from the answers and examples you give. This profile indicates quite a lot about your skill sets, attitude, and ability to cope in various situations.

> If the interviewer asks a question beginning with "Tell me about a time when"or "Can you give me an example?" you should immediately think: "Story."

Using Behavioral Answers

When the interview is completed, the interviewer or interviewers will rate your answers and examples and evaluate you by using some sort of rating system. A sample evaluation might look something like the one below, which uses a five-point system in which each answer receives a specific point value. Each interviewer will rate your performance on the basis of the impression he or she acquired from your examples and stories.

Behavioral Interviewing Scoring System

1. Much more than acceptable
   Past experience is significantly above criteria required for successful performance. (5 points)

2. More than acceptable
   Past experience generally exceeds criteria relative to quality and quantity of behavior required. (3 points)

3. Acceptable
   Past experience meets criteria relative to quality and quantity of behavior required. (2 points)

4. Less than acceptable
   Past experience generally does not meet criteria relative to quality and quantity of behavior required. (1 point)

5. Much less than acceptable
   Past experience is significantly below criteria required for successful job performance. (no points)

Each interviewer will add up the points awarded for each question, and a discussion will result (if the process has been done effectively). Your score is determined by what the interviewers hear in the answers you provide. If they are impressed by the stories you tell, they will rate you high: "much more than acceptable." If you have failed to give a specific example or back up your claims, they may rate you lower: "less than acceptable." The points will be tallied and compared.

What you tell them is the only evidence the hiring manager can use to judge you at this point. Therefore, the more relevant and recent your stories are, the more of an impact they will have on the interviewer. When no experiences are related or if they happened more than 10 years ago, your score will be low. If you fail to tell your stories in an interesting and convincing manner, you may be rated low even though you may have the past experience necessary to perform well in the job.

> Your stories and the way you relate them will be the key to convincing the interviewer that you are the right person for the job.

Your Ability to Show That You Can Do It Again

Candidates who prepare their success stories for behavioral interviews are able to answer the questions asked with greater ease and success compared with those who "wing" the interview. In fact, being fully prepared will even help you answer traditional interview questions. When you feel prepared, you will feel more confident and relaxed and will be able to connect with the interviewer more effectively.

The interviewer is listening for specific examples from you and stories about the way you performed in a similar job or role. If you were a marketing person and came up with an original idea for a new campaign, and if the campaign was successful and brought in new business, your story will have a great impact because the interviewer will be hopeful that you can repeat that success.

Because not every interviewer is trained in behavioral interviewing techniques, you may be asked more general or traditional questions such as "What are your strengths and weaknesses?" If you develop your past success stories fully (see Step 3 for more information), you will feel better prepared and more confident about talking about yourself and will be able to answer almost any type of question.

Some interviews will focus more on situational questions such as "What you would do *if* you encountered a situation such as…?" Here you essentially can make up an answer. Keep in mind, though, that even these answers will be stronger if you can give examples of times when you handled similar situations. The more information you can give the interviewer about yourself, the more accurate and reliable the picture of you that is being formed will be.

Listening to the Question Will Give You the Clue

Traditional Questions: "What Would You Do If…?"

When you are asked a question such as "What would you do if the following happened?" you can wing the answer. You have the option of quoting from information you've read or studied to answer the question. In other words, you can tell an interviewer about something about which you have no firsthand experience. You can spin a tale.

Interviewer's Question

"What is the first thing you would do if you were given this position?" (**Hint**: You know that this specific job requires the use of communication skills, so why not start there?)

Answer

First, I'd get to know the specific responsibilities of the other staff members. I'd talk with each of them and make sure that I learned what they did. Then I'd read as much as possible about the company and do research to learn what policies were implemented in the past. I'd also read the policy manual and find out the rules of the company. I'm sure that I would have a busy time just getting up to speed in the first 90 days or so.

There is really nothing wrong with this answer. It answers the question asked. The interviewer did not ask for a specific example or time. But note that the interviewer doesn't really get any concrete evidence of the way you work or the value of your skills at the conclusion of the answer. You gave a textbook answer, and that's all the interviewer has to go on when he or she judges whether you could do the job effectively and fit in at the company.

Behavioral Questions: "Tell Me About a Time When...."

When you hear a question that begins by asking for an example, you will know that something is required beyond a made-up answer. The interviewer is seeking information about your past behavior. In other words, she or he is asking for a "specific" example of a time when you dealt with a similar experience. If you give a general answer or fabricate an answer to this type of question, not only will that answer fail to answer the question, it may backfire when the interviewer begins to probe for more information.

When you hear a behavioral question, it's your cue that the interview is looking for an example of one of your specific experiences. Your answer should relate an incident in which you were involved. Here's an example.

Interviewer's Question:

"Tell me about a time when you started a new job and had to meet a group of people you'd never met before." (**Hint:** You know from the question that the interviewer is seeking to learn about a specific time when you began a new job.)

Answer

When I started my last job, one of the challenges that I faced was getting to know a group of people who were not very happy that I got the job because an internal person was hoping to get the position. So you might say that I had a hostile greeting.

I didn't let that bother me, as I had been in similar situations over the course of my career. The first thing I did was take a couple of days to get to know who did what and identify some of the people who needed special "handling." My boss was very helpful about filling me in and introducing me around the various departments.

Because I had to interface with several of the most hostile persons as part of my responsibilities, I set up appointments to meet with those people individually. When we had a meeting, one of the first things I told the person was that I was a team player, and I quoted some of the things my last team had said about me. I'm known for my partnering. My previous team members called me "Reliable Sam" because they knew I would come through for them in the clutch. This approach seemed to soften their attitude. I did a lot more listening than I did talking through the meetings and came away with a great deal of information and new confidence that I could work with this team. I made some promises to them in regard to some additional resources I could provide, and I made sure that I made good on each promise.

In the end, I won over each member within the month. I think my success was due to my waiting and not rushing in before I saw the lay of the land. My boss was really impressed with my ability to win them over.

The biggest difference between the answer to a traditional question and the answer to a behavioral question lies in the details and skills that are provided. The behavioral answer given above conveyed several skills to the interviewer: the ability to confront difficult situations or challenges, patience, planning, communication skills, an understanding of people's differences, listening skills, follow-through, courage, and commitment.

You can see the advantage of telling your story to convey your behavior: The interviewer gets a more accurate picture of you and learns about your skills and abilities and the ways you used them in the past. Remember that even when you are not asked behavioral questions, you can still use your stories by saying to the interviewer, "Let me tell you about a time when I solved a similar problem for my last employer."

Stories Demonstrating Your Skills

Your examples are best told through a story format. The more interesting and relevant your story is, the more the interviewer will want to hear further examples.

As we discussed above, a question that asks for "an example of a time" must address "a time" when you dealt with a situation. If you do not provide an example, you will fail to answer the question and will have missed an opportunity to relate what you have to bring to this job on the basis of your past successes.

Unless you have thought about this type of questioning ahead of time, you may find yourself caught off-guard and be unable to respond with the strongest answer on the spot. The challenge of answering these questions is to select the *right* story: the one that shows off your skills and abilities in the best possible manner. The problem is that you may have had many years of work experience and have solved lots of problems.

You may wonder about the following:

- *Which problem does this interviewer want to hear about?* Always relate to the job description/advertisement and what the employer is looking for. If the employer wants a focus on customer service, talk about the times when you had great success with the customers.

- *How much detail should I go into?* Detail is important as long as it is relevant. If the employer is looking for a problem solver and that is your particular strength, let the interviewer hear about your method of solving problems, such as analyzing, asking questions, trial and error, or whatever makes you a successful problem solver.

■ *What is this interviewer looking for?* The interviewer is looking for someone who can come in and do the work–solve the problems–someone who has had the past experiences or knowledge and knows how to make good judgments and work hard. Let the interviewer know what you have to bring; this includes your transferable skills and personal traits.

Preparing your examples before the interview will give you a head start in being able to provide answers to those questions. There is nothing worse than leaving an interview and regretting that you did not tell the interviewer about a time when you excelled. If you leave the interview and haven't given the interviewer a complete picture of "you," it will represent an opportunity that you cannot go back and repeat. Preparing your examples before the interview is essential to your success. Preparation will make or break your chances of convincing the interviewer that you have had the experience needed for this job. To prepare, think about your stories—and write them—before the interview. Doing this preparation enables you to select the stories that prove your claim that you are experienced. It is also an opportunity to demonstrate your skills and abilities through examples of past successes. When you prepare ahead of the interview, you can select the stories that show your abilities in the best light. The following material discusses the elements of a strong story. Once you've mastered these elements, the rest of the book will teach you how to prepare your own stories.

The Elements of Your Story

One of the first rules regarding answering behavioral questions is that they require a *complete* and *specific* example or story. The interviewer will have a much easier job listening to and following your stories if they are laid out in a chronological, easy-to-follow sequence of events. The most successful stories include the following elements:

Beginning: What the problem was

Middle: What you did about the problem

End: How it turned out

Let's examine each part of the story in the following example.

Interviewer's Question

"How did you successfully solve a problem in your past experience?"

Step 1: The clues in the question tell you that your answer should focus on a specific time when you solved a problem. The first thing you must do is let the interviewer know *what the problem was* by defining the problem or situation in a way that is to the point.

Answer's Beginning

I worked in the customer service department in my last company and was responsible for dealing with the escalated problem calls—basically people who were beyond complaining and were ready to cancel their orders. I was receiving lots of complaints from customers who were not able to get through to the customer service line to place their orders. The delay, or waiting period, sometimes was more than five minutes.

Here the problem is conveyed in a clear and concise manner. You have set the stage. The interviewer now knows what the problem was in the example you will be providing.

Step 2: Next, your answer should include action steps that make it clear to the interviewer *what you did about the problem.* In other words, what was your role? What skills did you use? What was your method of operation?

Answer's Middle

The first step I took was to find out why the problem existed. I interviewed the people who were taking orders and found out some of the problems they were encountering and the complaints they were hearing from customers.

I then analyzed my findings and determined that the problem was a lack of sufficient coverage during peak hours and too much coverage during downtimes.

I put together a small team to monitor and track calls and complaints.

When I received the data from the team, I did some research on tracking systems. I talked to other customer service people in various companies and made some phone calls to get quotes.

I wrote a proposal to my manager explaining the problem and made a recommendation to purchase a tracking system that would solve the problem.

I met with my manager and laid out the problem with data, facts, and quotes. She was receptive to what I had found and the solution I had come up with.

My manager and I then presented my report to upper management. I prepared a PowerPoint presentation that included a full report of the facts and figures and an estimate of the cost to improve the situation.

The interviewer has heard some valuable information about you through this specific example of your actions. Some of the skill sets you've revealed through your past actions include problem-solving skills, communication skills, listening skills, analytical skills, leadership skills, initiative, research skills, resourcefulness, writing skills, the ability to influence others, presentation skills, financial savvy, and the ability to interface with all levels of management.

You've presented your role, in this example walking through the specific steps you took to solve the problem. The interviewer is beginning to hear that you have the experience you claimed on your résumé. Remember, anyone can say that he or she is a good problem solver, but not everyone can give a specific example of a time when he or she solved a problem by providing specific details and facts as proof.

Step 3: The story is not finished until you relate the results, in other words, *how it turned out.*

Ending the story is very important. If you leave out the results, the interviewer will be left wondering, "What happened? How did it turn out?" Your answer should include any results or feedback you received.

Answer's End

Upper management was very impressed with my presentation. There was some budget tweaking, but we got the green light to move forward. The new system is now in place, and orders have increased by 25 percent during peak hours. My boss was really delighted with me for finding the solution and putting together such a thorough package. I received the customer service award of a night on the town. I was really pleased.

This ending wraps up the example by indicating what improvements were made and how the company benefited as a result of your efforts. In this case the company increased revenue through the use of a more efficient system. Note also that if you can quantify a result (a 25 percent increase in orders), it gives the interviewer the scope of your success. Another plus to this story was that it gave a quote or reaction from someone involved in the example: "My boss was really delighted." Any time you were rewarded, such as through a promotion, bonus, or award, that definitely should be included in your answer.

You can see from this example how much an interviewer can learn about the way you work from a single story. Because you structured the story chronologically, it's easier for the interview to understand the problem, your actions, and your results. Preparing your stories before the interview will allow you to put them in order and make a tremendous difference in your ability to make an impact during the interview.

Exercise: Putting Your Best Stories Forward

Think of a story you would like to tell an interviewer to let her or him know that you have had some past experiences. For this exercise identify a specific time when you did something that you were especially pleased about or were commended or rewarded for doing. It doesn't have to be a big success, just something that you think would be of interest to the interviewer. Construct the story in its three parts:

Step 1: Beginning: what the problem was. (Your examples must be specific, concise, and relevant to the question asked.)

Step 2: Middle: what you did about the problem. (Your examples should include *action*, demonstrating your role.)

Step 3: End: how it turned out. (Your stories must have results.)

Eliminate the Negative

Go through your story and make sure it shows you in the best light by eliminating the following negative traits:

- Your examples should not be *negative* or *whining*.
- Your examples should not *bad-mouth* anybody.
- Your examples should not be longer than *three minutes*.
- Your examples should not *ramble on* about irrelevant details.
- Your examples should not include *inappropriate* language or *slang*.
- Your answers should not involve *controversial* subjects.

Identifying the Key Factors of the Job

The Key Factors

Every job has key factors or competencies that people at the company have identified as necessary or desirable in the person they hire to perform the duties of the job. Before you can write your success stories, you must determine what those key factors are so that you can tailor your résumé and the words you use to sell yourself to fit the requirements of the job. Reading through job postings and advertisements is one of the most effective ways to find out what employers are seeking in a candidate.

One of the secrets in the direction of identifying these key factors is to begin to think like an interviewer. In the following sections you will learn to identify these factors. Your task will be to identify the key skills necessary to do the job as if you were the person making the hiring decisions.

You Are the Interviewer

Let's start by looking at a hypothetical job and deciding what key factors are desired for that job.

Example: Job Posting for a Market Manager

Under each description are the skills needed for each responsibility. After each description comes a list of five or six key factors to be used in the interview process. When you are looking at a job posting, remember to look beyond what is written and consider the personal traits and transferable skills you think will be needed to do this job.

Responsibilities of the Marketing Manager Position

Market managers are responsible for the gross profit in assigned markets and own inventory, cost, pricing, and merchandising decisions for that market.

1. Develop and maintain supplier relationships at the property and chain level through daily contact. Identifying skills needed:
   - Good communication skills
   - Listening skills
   - Ability to build customer relations
   - Interpersonal skills
   - Follow-through
   - Tracking
   - Organization

2. Analyze contracts and execute pricing. Skills needed:
   - Analytical ability
   - Some legal knowledge or experience
   - Negotiation skills
   - Ability to work with numbers
   - Knowledge of the competition/industry

3. Implement Extranet rate and inventory revisions, ensure suppliers understand Extranet, and increase supplier use of Extranet. Skills required:
   - Flexibility
   - Strong communication skills
   - Experience with customer service
   - Ability to influence sales

4. Conduct weekly competitive analysis for key markets, report findings, and make adjustments. Skills needed:
   - Analytical skills
   - Ability to read data and take action
   - Ability to see bigger picture

5. Monitor, evaluate, and report on progress of individual accounts and markets toward achieving weekly, monthly, and annual targets. Skills needed:

- Ability to make decisions
- Good analytical skills
- Goal-oriented
- Motivation
- Organization
- Ability to keep finger on accounts

6. Understand key market hard/soft periods, know destinations and trends, create and maintain event calendars for key market locations, and plan courses of action required to meet supply, demand, and necessary sales. Skills required:

- Business savvy
- Future-oriented thinking
- Ability to keep abreast of the industry/economy/customer's needs
- Ability to plan, organize, and implement
- Ability to take plans forward

7. Execute annual contract negotiations. Skills required:

- Communication skills
- Negotiation skills
- Knowledge of contract law

Qualifications Listed by Employer

- College degree or minimum of three years of account management experience in hotel industry. Strong organization, communication, and people skills required
- Team player
- Working knowledge of account and inventory management preferred. Proficiency in Microsoft Word and Excel
- Ability to work and thrive in a multitask, fast-paced environment
- Professional, get-it-done attitude and work ethic

Six Suggested Key Factors

1. **Communication:** including good people and listening skills
2. **Adaptability:** ability to handle multiple tasks
3. **Ability to influence:** customer focus—relationship building, selling
4. **Negotiation/numbers ability**
5. **Analytical problem solving:** analysis of data
6. **Big picture thinking:** results-focused

Summary of Skills Desired for This Position to Be Used in Job Posting

Marketing Manager Position: An experienced, outgoing, high-energy person with good communication skills who is analytical and confident. Someone who thinks "beyond today"—a visionary who can make things happen.

Job postings/job descriptions are like pieces of gold; mine them carefully for the words they contain.

Exercise: Identifying Key Factors

Now it's your turn to practice identifying the key factors or competencies. Find a posting or advertisement that interests you and select the key factors and competencies needed to do the job. Don't limit yourself geographically for this exercise. The only qualifier is that you would be interested in this job.

What Are They Looking For?

What are the qualifications listed?

- _____
- _____
- _____
- _____
- _____

What do you see that is needed? This may require you to read between the lines.

- _____
- _____
- _____
- _____
- _____

Condense the factors you've identified into five or six words (i.e., *communication, adaptable, ability to influence, leadership*).

- 1. _____
- 2. _____
- 3. _____
- 4. _____
- 5. _____
- 6. _____

Note: These are the words and skills that should be emphasized on your résumé and in the interview to show that you are a perfect match for the position.

What Do You Have to Offer?

Knowledge-Based Skills

Some interviewers place the greatest emphasis on your knowledge and experience. Although this is not the best way to hire, it is a common practice. These skills usually are defined clearly in the job posting.

Take some time to identify your knowledge-based skills: Here are some examples:

Analyzing

Estimating

Coordinating

Negotiating

Organizing

Public speaking

Mechanical adeptness

Leadership skills

Counseling

Artistic skills

Computer skills

Entrepreneurial skills

Design skills

Budgeting skills

Training skills

Project management skills

Transferable Skills

Transferable skills are portable. In other words, you can take them with you to almost any job.

Identifying transferable skills is especially important for anyone who is transferring to another field or type of organization. Think about what you have to offer in the way of transferable skills Chances are that you are taking for granted some of the skills that make you unique.

List your transferable or portable skills. Here are some examples: Communication, Planning, Negotiation, Organizational skills, Time management, Problem solving, Customer service, Teaching, Coaching, Follow-through, Resourcefulness.

Make up your own list:

- _____
- _____
- _____
- _____
- _____
- _____
- _____
- _____
- _____

Personal Skills

Personal skills are the qualities that make you unique—who you are. These are skills that cannot be taught even though employers would like to do that. These skills are very important to outstanding job performance but sometimes are undervalued by both the candidate and the interviewer.

Think about your personal traits. Here are some examples: Flexible, Friendly, Dependable, Good attitude, Reliable, Calm, High energy, Patient, Self-starter, Organized, Quick learner, People oriented, Goal-directed, Good sense of humor.

Make up your own list:

- _____
- _____
- _____
- _____
- _____
- _____

Exercise: The Three Ps

Divide a piece of paper into three columns and label them with the headings "Previous Experience," "Portable Skills," and "Personality Traits." Like the three Ps of marketing, this will be your marketing tool.

Education and Previous Experience

(Examples: vendor management, product development, computer expertise/knowledge)

- _____
- _____
- _____
- _____

Portable/Transferable Skills

(Examples: customer relations, communications, ability to coordinate, problem solving, time management)

- _____
- _____
- _____
- _____
- _____
- _____
- _____

Personality Traits

(Examples: self-starter, independent, friendly, organized, quick learner, good attitude)

- _____
- _____
- _____
- _____
- _____
- _____

When you finish, check the list to see a summary of what you have to offer. You may be surprised when you see how easily the list comes together. When you divide the skills, the task becomes manageable.

Take the key factors you identified from the job posting and compare them with what you have to offer. The next step is to plan a strategy to show off those traits in the stories and the answers you will prepare for the interview questions. It is now time to organize and prepare your stories involving past experiences so that when the time comes for the interview, you will convince the people making the hiring decisions that you are the best person for the job.

Writing Your Success Stories by Using Key Factors

Stories to Fit the Key Factors of the Job

Storytelling consists of relating an incident or entertaining an audience with a tale. Some people consider storytelling an "art form." To expand on that theme, and using movie plots as an example of how a story unfolds to capture and hold the audience's attention, this chapter will show how the art of telling stories can be most effective.

By analyzing movie plots you can see that almost all stories have a basic format that begins with a problem or obstacle, sometimes a formidable one. Then, at some point, usually in the first few minutes of the movie, the plot starts to thicken and the action begins. This is the part in which the characters attempt to deal with a situation or solve a problem, usually with some trials and tribulations and steps taken to move the plot forward while details are given to hold the viewers' attention. All good stories must have an ending: something that leaves the viewer with a feeling, positive or negative. The ending is always crucial to the story so that a solution can be seen—and in many cases a triumph over challenge can be achieved. You can use the same format to relate your professional success stories.

Using the plot of the classic movie *The Wizard of Oz* as an example, let's examine how the storytelling process might work in your job search:

- *The beginning of the movie (the problem):* In the first 30 seconds of the movie a problem is identified: A wicked woman (who turns into a witch) is chasing after Dorothy (the heroine) and her dog, Toto. Dorothy must protect her dog at all costs.

- *The plot or middle (the action):* Dorothy has quite an adventure, full of challenges and obstacles, working with a strange bunch of characters. There are several twists and turns, along with challenges to overcome and survive.
- *The ending (The result):* Dorothy survives and returns home, helping several others along the way.

You can see how this plot develops with a beginning, a middle, and an end. This is the way your interview stories should evolve. Using Dorothy as a job hunter, we'll show how her adventures prove that she is the right person for the job.

Ad in the Local Newspaper

WANTED—Experienced adventurer extraordinaire. Seeking a high-energy person to lead a diverse team on an unusual quest to achieve multiple goals. Must have excellent communication skills and a great imagination. Ability to be resourceful and determined is essential. Also must love animals.

Dorothy applies for the job that she knows she can handle as a result of her recent experience and success. She lands an interview because of her outstanding résumé. Dorothy is smart and does some preinterview preparation. The first thing she does is put together a list of key factors necessary to do the job, which she determines by analyzing the job ad. She carefully reads and thinks about what it will take to do this job. As you did in Step 2, she reads between the lines and identifies six key factors:

- *Adaptable:* must have experience adapting to new situations and challenges
- *Team player:* ability to work with diverse teams
- *Resourceful:* good problem-solving skills—the ability to think outside the box
- *Leadership:* must be able to take the lead in overcoming and dealing with obstacles

- *Determined:* does not give up in spite of the odds
- *Communication skills:* concern for people and animals

Dorothy prepares her stories and feels that she will be able to relate them to the interviewer as proof that she has what it takes to do the job. She feels prepared and confident as she enters the interviewer's office.

One of the first interview questions asked is "Tell me about a time when you led an adventure with a team."

Dorothy is ready with her answer:

- *Problem:* I recently had quite an adventure going through the land of Oz. There was a hostile woman who was after me and my dog, meaning us harm. My only recourse was to plan an escape for both of us and then eventually find my way back home.

- *Action:* The first thing I did was obtain information from a beautiful and good witch I met upon my arrival in Oz. She told me to follow the yellow brick road, which I did. During my travels I encountered potential team members on the road. Each team member had his own agenda, but we agreed on a common goal: to see the Wizard. I led the team by explaining the plan and using my resources whenever possible, including dousing the wicked witch with water and destroying her in the process. As a team we had to overcome several obstacles, such as trees that threw apples, flying monkeys, and sleep-inducing poppies. I remained cool and calm in the face of some rather distressing situations. I never stopped believing that we could achieve our goal. There were times when the team members lost faith and began to doubt. I was able to boost morale by having them focus on the end result: achieving their dreams. I was in constant contact with my team members, supporting and encouraging them when needed.

- *Result:* Even though each team member had his own agenda, I am happy to report that we all achieved our goals. If you were to talk to my team members, they would tell you that they were very unhappy to see me leave my position as leader. I was especially touched when one of them told me, "I would never have found my dream if it hadn't been for you." As for myself, I was able to get my dog and me home safely, but I also found an inner power that I didn't know I had. It was an awesome experience, and I now have new values that are important to me. I know I am very well qualified as a guide and leader and could go out there and lead another team successfully.

The interviewer is impressed with Dorothy and the skills described in this story.

- *Adaptable:* adjusted to the new land almost immediately and set out on the suggested road
- *Team player:* supported other team members' quests from the start
- *Resourceful:* found the yellow brick road and doused the wicked witch with water to destroy her
- *Leadership:* assumed the role of leader from the beginning and was steadfast
- *Determined:* was a survivor in spite of overwhelming odds, such as trees, monkeys, and poppies
- *Communication skills:* was in constant contact with team members, encouraging them when needed

By relating her earlier success stories, Dorothy has let the interviewer know about the skills she can bring to the job. Using additional prepared stories, Dorothy is able to prove to the interviewer that she is the best person for the job. Her past behavior is an indicator of her future success, and she is hired!

From Dorothy's experience you can see that preparation does pay off. A well-told example helps the interviewer match your qualifications to his or her needs. The interviewing process gives you an opportunity to tell your stories and your triumphs over challenges so that the interviewer can use patterns of behavior to determine whether you have what it takes to get the job done. The main objective of the story is to relate your strengths and skills through past experiences and behaviors. The more interesting and relevant to the job your stories are, the more impressive they will be at demonstrating that you have been there and done that—and can do it again.

Begin to think of your stories as "tales" of past experiences. All good tales have a beginning, a middle, and an ending.

The beginning: Once upon a time… (the situation)

The middle: The plot, the action and steps taken, the challenges and obstacles

The ending: The outcome (how it turned out)

Using Acronyms as a Guide

One of the challenges of writing and telling success stories is to tell them in a succinct and organized manner. Your story should unfold in a chronological sequence, making it easy for the listener to follow it and learn additional information about you and the way you work.

You may be familiar with the concept of using an acronym—the first letter of each word in a series—to remember items in a sequential manner. For example, Mother's Against Drunk Driving can be shortened to MADD. The acronym not only gives your memory a jog but also provides a format and structure for you to follow. When it comes to interviewing, several acronyms are used to tell stories, some of which you may have encountered in other books you have read or courses you have attended. Some of the more commonly used acronyms in storytelling are the following:

CAB

    Challenge: What was the problem you had to overcome?
    Action: What techniques and skills did you use to accomplish your goal?
    Behavior: What was the behavior relative to this situation?

PAR

    Problem: Why you did it
    Action: What you did
    Result: What the outcome was

SAR

    Situation: What was the problem?
    Action: What steps did you take?
    Result: What was the result?

STAR

    Situation/Task: the background of the action
    Action: the response—what was done
    Result: the effects of the actions

SBO

    Situation: the situation you encountered
    Behavior: the behavior used
    Outcome: the way it turned out—successes/failures

SAO

    Situation: description of the situation
    Action: actions taken by you
    Outcome: the results

SPARE

    Situation/Problem: succinct description of the challenge
    Action: the detailed role taken by you
    Result: the results, rewards, and comments received
    Enthusiasm: your reaction to or feeling about the situation

The common pattern in these acronyms is the chronological order they use to relate the events:

- *A beginning:* the reason for the story—the why
- *A middle:* the action or plot of the story—the how
- *A conclusion:* the result—the outcome

The Proportions of a Story

These acronyms can be used as a template when you are writing or telling your stories, but it is important to understand that you should use certain proportions to get the impact you want.

You may have noticed when you were answering the questions in the Interview IQ Test that some of the answers were not as strong as others were because the emphasis was in the wrong place. In other words, the stories were out of proportion. Some of the stories placed too much emphasis on the problem and not enough on the action. Some had a good beginning and middle but lacked a conclusion or outcome. By breaking down the story into specific proportions, you will keep the focus on your *skills and experiences,* not on the company or the problem.

> The point of employing an acronym in storytelling is have a tool to use in writing and telling stories so that they are clearer, more focused, and more sequential.

Anatomy of a Story

A common mistake candidates make is not giving enough detail in the action part of the story. If you do not include the action steps or the details of what you did, the listener cannot get a clear picture of the skill sets you used to achieve the result. By spending too much time on the beginning or the ending you are missing an opportunity to let interviewers know that you have done what they are looking for in similar situations in your earlier jobs.

Common Problems Encountered in Answering Behavioral Questions

- Too much time is given to setting up the story.
- Not enough information is provided in the middle of the story. The action is simplified, making it sound like an easy task or problem when in fact it was very difficult and involved a great deal of effort above and beyond the norm.
- The story does not have an ending. What was the outcome? The interviewer is left wondering, "What happened next?"

Your Story

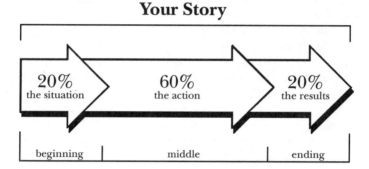

Model Proportions

The beginning—20 percent or less: the situation, task, or problem

The middle—60 percent or more: the action, the steps taken to solve the problem: ideas generated, tasks performed, challenges overcome (your role in the process)

The ending—20 percent or less: the results: cost savings, bonuses, awards, promotions (the outcome)

Examples of Story Proportions

Using the correct proportions for a story is essential in getting your points across in a succinct manner. When you spend too much or too little time on one part, the story does not have the power it could have. Below are two examples of behavioral questions and answers. One is a poor example, and the other is a good example.

A Poorly Told Story

Interviewer's Question

"Tell me about a time when you dealt with a dissatisfied customer."

Beginning: That is the nature of my job: dealing with dissatisfied customers. I probably get an average of 25 calls each day from people who aren't satisfied with the products, have a broken part, want information on how to return the product, or need information about how to operate the product. They call and yell at us, thinking it is our responsibility. It's like they think we are empowered to do something about the problem. We have a policy at ABC to always try to satisfy the customer.

Middle: No action

End: We even go so far as to refund money in some cases. Other companies would not be so generous, but our company really cares about its reputation.

This story has problems with the proportions and as a result lacks order and effectiveness:

- Too much emphasis is on the problem/situation (more than 20 percent of the story).
- No identifiable skills are given (no action).
- The end is focused on what the company does, not on the skills and knowledge you possess.

A Well-Told Story

Interviewer's Question

"Tell me about a time when you dealt with a dissatisfied customer."

Beginning: A female customer called one day with a complaint about an order we had shipped incorrectly. She was very upset and started yelling at me.

Middle: The first thing I did was listen very carefully and let her vent. I talked to her in a quiet tone, making sure I was polite but not condescending. When she had calmed down, I asked her to explain the details of the situation. I then repeated the problem back to her and confirmed that I understood all the details. I assured her that I would call her back that day. I did some research on the problem and the circumstances. After I had the facts, I discussed the situation with my supervisor. I made a recommendation that we adjust the customer's bill on the basis of my findings, and my supervisor agreed.

End: I called the woman back that day, as promised, and told her what we could do to make it up to her. She was very receptive to our offer and felt satisfied with the adjustment. She asked to speak to my supervisor and told her about my excellent and professional customer service.

You don't have to be a trained interviewer to see the difference between these two stories. The first story is very vague and incomplete, with too little emphasis on the action and too much emphasis on the beginning (the problem). The interviewer will have a difficult time judging what the candidate has to offer at the conclusion of this story. What skills could you pick out? Not many.

The second story is very specific and points out several qualities an interviewer is looking for in an employee who will be dealing with customers. The story is easy to follow and has appropriate proportions: 20 percent for the beginning, 60 percent for the middle, and 20 percent for the ending.

Exercise: Identifying Skills

Reread the second story and identify the skills you can draw from it. List them below:

_____

_____

_____

_____

Here are some of the skills in the well-told story:

Good listening skills

Communication skills

Follow-through

Research

Fact-finding skills

Initiative

Problem-solving skills

If you were the interviewer and picked out these skills, would you want to hear more from this candidate? Probably you would, especially if these are the skills you identified as important to the position.

Once you feel comfortable with the concept and proportions of story-telling, try retaking the Interview IQ Test to improve your score.

Your Success Stories

Writing success stories is one of the most important steps in preparing for an interview. The first step in the process is to determine which factors are crucial to the position for which you are applying (you learned how to do this in Step 2). Once you have determined the skills and competencies that are required, the next step is to write your own experience stories that emphasize those factors.

A common problem in writing stories involves the use of pronouns. You easily can get tangled in pronouns and miss out on the opportunity to explain your role in the story. When you use too many "we"s, it is difficult, if not impossible, for the interviewer to know "your" role in the situation. Here is an example: "*We* had a problem with the database *we* were working on, and *we* had to do a quick analysis to determine the cause. The first thing *we* did was analyze the previous data. *We* found the flaw within a few minutes, and *we* were able to solve the problem in record time."

This example has six "we"s and no "I"s. What was your role? You got lost in the example somewhere. There is no proof of *your* performance in the story; this means that you have missed an opportunity to show the interviewer your skill sets.

If you are worried about using the pronoun "I" too many times, talk about the team you worked with but at the same time include your role and what you did. Here is an example:

I worked with a team, and my role was to do the analysis on the product. We got together, and each person presented his or her findings. I found that there was a basic error in the system and was able to work with the engineer to reconfigure the problem.

The strong point in this story is that there is a sense of what your role was on the team. You didn't take the credit for the solution but showed that you played a role in the solution.

Exercise: The Story Line

It is now time for you to write your own success stories so that you can let the interviewer know you are the best person for the job.

Step 1. The first step is to determine which factors are crucial to the position. Once you have determined what skills and competencies are required, you can begin to write experience stories that address your experience in the identified areas.

Here is an example:

- Communication
- Decision making
- Initiative
- Planning and organizing
- Flexibility
- Leadership

Step 2. On the basis of these requirements, formulate at least two possible questions for each of the six factors. (Refer to tThe Interview IQ Test for examples of questions.)

Some sample questions include the following:

"Tell me about a time when your communication skills made a difference in the outcome of a project."

"Can you give me an example of a time when you had to break down complex terms into simple language to communicate to a group?"

Step 3. For each key factor or job requirement, prepare at least two stories that illustrate your successes and answer the questions you have formulated.

Step 4. Review your stories to see which examples are interchangeable and can be used to answer more than one direct question.

Exercise: *Your* Stories

Inr this exercise you'll be writing out your own stories, making sure the story proportions are right. You may find it easier to do this exercise if you use the acronym SPARE.

Situation or Problem: The
Beginning (20 Percent or Less)

What is the basis of the story? State the situation or problem at the beginning of the story. This part should be brief and concise.

There was a time when I encountered a problem with

_____

_____

Action or Behavior: The Middle (60 Percent or More)

Describe what *you* did to address the problem. List your actions. (Beware of the pronoun "we," which can take attention away from your part in the action). This part of the story should include movement and details.

I worked with a team, and my role was …

_____

_____

Some of the steps I took were …

_____

_____

The biggest challenge on this project was …

_____

_____

And then I …

_____

_____

Result: The End or Outcome (20 Percent or Less)

What was the outcome or ending to the story? Focus on your role in the project and any feedback you received.

The result was …

_____

_____

The feedback I received was ...

_____

_____

_____

Enthusiasm

End with some comments about your reaction to or feelings regarding the success of the situation or task.

The most rewarding part of this situation was ...

_____

_____

_____

The biggest challenge for me was ...

_____

_____

_____

What Not to Say

Ideally, your stories will demonstrate your abilities and successes. When you have been involved in a project that did not turn out the way it was planned but the end results had nothing to do with your performance (e.g., money ran out, customer canceled the order), you should focus on your role and how you fulfilled your task in the project. In other words, focus on what you were responsible for and how that part turned out.

Important Details to Include and
Unimportant Details to Exclude

Some of the ugly details of a story can be skipped over without taking attention away from your role in the situation. It is important to focus on the positive as much as possible during an interview.

It is in your best interest not to say anything negative about a company or boss in your stories. Remember, these are professional stories and you are demonstrating that you are a professional and the best person for the job.

Your stories should be as upbeat and interesting as possible. From the interviewer's perspective, hiring a new employee can be a very intense and somewhat tedious task. It is a task that a lot of managers would rather not have to perform because it involves talking to a great many people and listening to their experiences and the details of those experiences. However, when someone comes into the interview and begins to tell interesting stories, the interview becomes enjoyable and sometimes even fun. By engaging the interviewer with your stories, you will have a better chance of being remembered and thought of as a serious candidate for the job.

Your vocabulary and the words you use will tell the interviewer a lot about you. Be sure to familiarize yourself with the jargon of the industry. This will allow you to discuss problems and issues in a more intelligent manner.

The more at ease you are with what the interviewer is seeking and the closer a match you are to what the employer is looking for, the better chance you have of being selected.

Section 4
Understanding the Keys to Success

Preparation

As has been stressed throughout Part II, preparation *will* make a definite difference in your presentation for and confidence in taking an interview. One of the biggest mistakes job hunters make is not preparing well enough for a job interview. You must convey confidence about your skills and ability to do the job to let the interviewer know that you are the best person for the job.

The most successful interviews are ones that are conversational, involving an exchange between two professionals. For some people this may entail a paradigm shift in the way they think about an interview. However, if you do think in this new way, you will see greater results, experience a significant gain in confidence, have less fear, and get over some of your nervousness about the process. In an interview the worst possible position for a candidate to take is "Please, please, hire me." This not only is a weak and passive position, it also renders you powerless, and it is boring for the interviewer. Taking the following steps will help you gain greater confidence and give stronger answers.

Step 1: Stop thinking of the interview process as a hockey game and begin thinking of it as a two-way conversation between two professionals.

Step 2: Start thinking of the process as a business solution process in which the employer has a problem and you, the candidate, are the solution to that problem.

> The necessary paradigm shift in the interview process entails changing from the defensive position of responding to questions with the answers you think the interviewer wants to hear to thinking of the process as two or more people getting together to check each other out.

Centering your preparation on you as a product and what that product has to offer will change the focus of your preparation and presentation. To prepare for interviews, use the Interview IQ Test as a guide and complete all the exercises in this book. Doing that will give you a much stronger sense of what you have to offer and what makes you unique so that you can sell yourself on the basis of what you can offer the employer.

A self-assessment of your skills and traits is essential before you can think about yourself as a product. The more details you have about your skill sets, the more effectively you will be able to present yourself as the solution to the employer's problem (i.e., the best person for the job). List not only your knowledge and experience from former positions but also some of your transferable skills as well as your personal traits, which are important factors for success in any job. By identifying the key factors of the position and then basing your stories on the competencies identified, you will be taking the *most essential* step in your preparation. Focusing that preparation on what the employer is seeking will make a big difference in the way you communicate, especially when it comes to asking questions. By printing out several postings (the only criterion being that you would be interested in applying, not that you necessarily will), you will begin to be familiar with the requirements of the jobs in your field as well as the vocabulary used. Take the words and use them to enhance your credibility. The words you use to express yourself send a strong message about who you are and what you know. Your vocabulary and how well you use it say more about you than does the message you're trying to communicate.

Practice, Practice, Practice

Interviewing is a learned skill. As with any other skill or learned technique, the more you practice, the more you will improve. You will find that receiving objective feedback on how you are coming across will help you be more effective. When you can listen objectively to any advice or critique you receive, you will learn a lot about the impression you are making. No one likes being criticized, but this is a time when you need to know whether you are sending the right message and making the impression you intend to make. Here are some methods to use for getting feedback. Keep in mind that some may be more effective for you than others are.

Actual Interviews

Using interviews to get feedback is a method that can be very costly. You can use job interviews that are not of great importance as practice if you have the opportunity, but that can backfire if you discover that this would be a better opportunity for your career than you originally thought. You may discover that when you are not concerned about whether you get the job, you may interview at your best because you don't have anything to lose. Take that attitude toward interviews for jobs that you really want and you will have greater success.

Feedback is important, but getting the interviewer to give you feedback after you have been turned down is not easy. Most interviewers are concerned about saying the wrong thing and ending up being subject to some kind of a discrimination claim. Every once in a while someone will take the time to tell you where you could have been more effective and convincing. If you are fortunate enough to receive this type of feedback, keep an open mind and listen as objectively as possible. Learn from the experience.

Self-Coaching

Tape-record and listen to yourself. Although this technique may be challenging, try to be as objective as possible about what you hear. Try putting the tape away for a day or so before you play it back; this will help you be more objective. When you are ready, listen to the tape with an open mind. While you listen, ask yourself, "If I were the interviewer, would I hire me?"

Career Centers

If you have access to a career center through a school, government-sponsored organization, or private organization, take the opportunity to work with trained professionals who will give you feedback about the impression you are making.

Practice with a Friend or Family Member

This is a good way to practice as long as some ground rules have been established. However, it can be a disaster if it is not handled correctly. People who are close to you are often not in a good position to critique your performance as objectively as would someone who doesn't know you. Your friends and family members are emotionally involved and on your side. They may not want to say anything negative about your interviewing skills. Make sure to agree beforehand that the session will be limited to objective advice and then try to listen without taking it personally and getting your feelings hurt.

Professional Coaching

Use a coach, but not just any coach. Make sure she or he has had interview training, particularly in behavioral interviewing techniques. Qualify the coach by asking about the last time he or she was on an interview and his or her experiences as an interviewer. Make sure the coach has sat on both sides of the desk and ask for references from past clients.

Whatever method you choose, it is essential to practice, practice, and practice some more. Any feedback you receive should be listened to in as objective a mind-set as possible. This is not a time to be aggressive and argumentative. Don't take it personally but instead learn from the experience. Your goal should be to sound not rehearsed but prepared and natural.

Feeling Prepared = Improved Confidence = Successful Interviews = Job Offers

There are so many factors behind the scenes of the hiring process, it is impossible to judge why one interview ends in a job offer and one does not. What is possible to predict is that if you go to an interview and try to wing your answers, you will be less focused and feel less confident and will give the interviewer a weak picture of you.

Feeling confident is the most important trait you can show at an interview. If you believe in yourself and know you can do the job, you will be able to project that confidence. If you use phrases such as "pretty good," "think I can," and "probably could," you will not convince the interviewer that you are "the best person for the job." This is *not* a time to be modest; it is a time to sell yourself as the solution to the problem. Any statement you make should be made with conviction.

Interviewer's Question

"What makes you think you can do this job?"

Answer

I am a good match for this position and have the traits you are looking for. Through my past experiences I have encountered the challenges necessary to do this job. I am known for my ability to learn quickly and come up to speed in record time. I know I can make a difference in this department. I haven't set a goal yet that I didn't achieve. I've been there and done that—and can do it again for you!"

The Interview IQ Test gives you a look at the interviewing process from the other side of the desk. It is your entry into the world of the interviewer. The strength of the answers given there will help you gauge the effectiveness of your answers. Use the test as a learning tool and guide and use it over and over. Learn from the mistakes of the weaker answers as well as from the strengths of the stronger answers.

By taking the Interview IQ Test several times and perhaps reviewing it before every interview, you will have a stronger sense of what an interviewer is seeking when he or she says, "Give me an example of a time when...." By familiarizing yourself with behavioral interviewing techniques, you will be prepared to back your claims even when you are not asked for an example.

Once you have done the exercises and prepared your own stories, you will have a passport to successful interviewing. It will be up to you to prepare and practice until you have the skill perfected and are ready to go out to the next interview with cool, calm, and confidence.

Rules of Behavioral Interviewing

- Your examples must be *specific.*
- Your examples should be *concise.*
- Your examples should include *action.*
- Your examples must demonstrate *your role.*
- Your examples should be *relevant* to the questions asked.
- Your stories must have *results.*

Boost your Interview IQ and show the interviewer that you are the best person for the job!

Index

About the Author

Carole Martin is a professional interviewer and coach. In addition to having her own business, she has been an interview expert and a contributing writer at Monster.com for the past three years. Her unique background includes over 15 years of human resources management experience and a master's degree in career management. She has worked in technical and nontechnical industries, in Fortune 500 companies as well as in start-up companies.

She teaches and coaches interviewing skills at two universities, UC Berkeley's Haas School of Business and John F. Kennedy University.

Her work has extended worldwide as she has coached people through one-on-one and group workshops, in person, or by phone. She is an outplacement workshop presenter for individuals who have been laid off from their jobs. She also consults for companies in the San Francisco Bay Area, interviewing candidates to find the best person for the job.

Her favorite interview motto is:

Preparation = Self Confidence = Successful Interviews = Job Offers

For more information about Carole's services, see her Web site at: http://www.interviewcoach.com